W9-CIK-585

# stylish storage

# stylish storage

### simple ways to contain your clutter

paige gilchrist

LARK BOOKS

A Division of Sterling Publishing Co., Inc.
New York, NY

**PAIGE GILCHRIST**
editor

**CHRIS BRYANT**
art director
content stylist

**EVAN BRACKEN**
photography

**ORRIN LUNDGREN**
illustrations

**HEATHER SMITH**
assistant editor

**RAIN NEWCOMB**
editorial assistant

**HANNES CHAREN**
production assistance

**SPECIAL PHOTOGRAPHY**
VNU Syndication
Alexander van Berge
Henk Brandsen
Dennis Brandsma
Frank Brandwijk
John Dummer
Jerzy Frigge
Luuk Geertsen
Rene Gonkel
John van Groenedaal
Paul Grootes
Peter Kooijman
Robert Mulder
Otto Polman
Dolf Straatemeier
Joyce Vloet
George v.d. Wijngaard
Hans Zeegers

Library of Congress Cataloging-in-Publication Data

Gilchrist, Paige
   Stylish storage : simple ways to contain your clutter / by Paige Gilchrist.
      p.   cm.
   Includes index.
   ISBN 1-57990-237-5
   1. Storage in the home.   I. Title.

TX309.G55  2001
648'.8—dc21                                              2001029391
   CIP

10 9 8 7 6 5 4 3 2 1
First Edition

Published by Lark Books, a division of Sterling Publishing Co., Inc.,
387 Park Avenue South, New York, N.Y. 10016

© 2001, Lark Books

Distributed in Canada by Sterling Publishing, c/o Canadian Manda Group,
One Atlantic Ave., Suite 105, Toronto, Ontario, Canada M6K 3E7

Distributed in the U.K. by: Guild of Master Craftsman Publications Ltd.
Castle Place, 166 High Street, Lewes, East Sussex, England, BN7 1XU
Tel: (+ 44) 1273 477374 • Fax: (+ 44) 1273 478606
Email: pubs@thegmcgroup.com • Web: www.gmcpublications.com

Distributed in Australia by Capricorn Link (Australia) Pty Ltd.,
P. O. Box 704, Windsor, NSW 2756, Australia

The written instructions, photographs, designs, patterns, and projects in this volume are intended for the personal use of the reader and may be reproduced for that purpose only. Any other use, especially commercial use, is forbidden under law without written permission of the copyright holder.

Every effort has been made to ensure that all the information in this book is accurate. However, due to differing conditions, tools, and individual skills, the publisher cannot be responsible for any injuries, losses, and other damages that may result from the use of the information in this book.

If you have questions or comments about this book, please contact:
Lark Books
50 College Street
Asheville, NC 28801
(828) 253-0467

Manufactured in Hong Kong by Dai Nippon Printing, Ltd

All rights reserved

ISBN 1-57990-237-5

# contents

# introduction

THERE ARE BOOKS OUT THERE THAT PROPOSE elaborate schemes for storage systems throughout your home. They come complete with detailed checklists and lots of diagrams. They may also come with a warning that if you don't adopt their complex approach to storage, you'll suffer through a life of eternal disorganization.

This is not one of those books.

There are also books that suggest all you need to live a life of organized bliss is a home that features one-of-a-kind built-in shelving, customized nooks and crannies, and expansive walk-in closets equipped with expensive storage gadgetry. (Step one: win a large cash prize and build a new, larger home.)

This is not one of those books, either.

What this book *is* is an accessible, inspirational guide for real people (with real houses, real budgets, and busy lives) who want practical, easy ideas for containing some of the clutter those busy lives generate. Yes, you'll want to do some basic assessing of your needs before you rush out and buy stackable baskets and drawer organizers. But the simple planning process we've outlined for doing so is pretty painless—and appealingly logical. And yes, some of the storage solutions that best meet certain needs require a bit of hammering, stitching, or other basic do-it-yourself skills, but many other fixes are super quick—and nearly effortless.

Most of all, this is a book based on the real motivation behind more efficient storage: making your home a more beautiful place. If you find it hard to get excited about setting up utility shelves in the garage or stacking cardboard boxes in a closet, you're not alone. (And if that's your idea of storage, no wonder you've been putting it off.) Sure you want a place for everything. But while you're at it, you want to create a more attractive, inviting living space, one that reflects your personal style. We focus on storage solutions that help you do just that.

We've included clever ways to contain the ordinary and the frequently used (check out the simple stacked bricks that hold toothbrushes, page 124). We also offer imaginative solutions to universal storage problems (see the hotel towel rack that becomes an innovative approach to bedside storage, page 86). Plus, we've filled the book with inspirational ideas for maximizing the storage potential of every room (from easy-to-add molding that creates a ledge for storage or display, page 76, to tips for selecting storage-friendly furniture, page 70).

You can implement many of the ideas described on the following pages by simply adapting ordinary items you already own, whether you transform a ladder into a bathroom towel rack or a mirror and some interesting knobs and handles into a place for hanging jewelry and scarves. Other ideas show you creative ways to use pieces you can easily find, from flea-market furniture and commercially available organizers to basic baskets and boxes. Finally, if you want to build, sew, or otherwise assemble a few from-scratch storage options, we provide easy instructions for making basic wooden shelves, fabric hanging bags, and other pieces you can customize to meet your needs.

Whichever route you choose, you'll be inspired to take a fresh look at every object you own and where you might put it—and relieved to learn how easy it is to create the perfect place.

# storage basics

LET'S ACKNOWLEDGE RIGHT OFF THE BAT THAT THE TERM SYSTEM, AS IN STORAGE SYSTEM, IS A SOMEWHAT OFF-PUTTING ONE. It has the ring of something that takes planning sessions and charts to come up with. Worse yet, it sounds like something you're going to have to force yourself (not to mention others) to adhere to.

You'll be relieved to know that, in our book, a storage system can be (and often is) as uncomplicated as a vintage washtub that holds quilts in the bedroom or a trunk that hides blankets and board games under its lid in the living room. None of the ideas on the following pages require extensive planning or reorganizing to implement. All, however, are meant to be adapted to suit your specific needs. That adapting is what makes them effective storage solutions as opposed to decorative ideas that don't really work. So, before you rush out and implement any of them, first think through how to tailor them to your situation and style. The following process tells you how.

## identify your storage needs

Here's where you define the scope of the storage dilemma you're willing to tackle right now. You can be as focused as: *We need a place to store magazines other than all over the coffee table*, or as ambitious as: *I want this kitchen clutter-free once and for all.*

This is an important diving-in point, because it lets you set your boundaries. Maybe you're not ready to take on the whole living room right now, toys and video games and all. Perhaps the only storage problem you're prepared to face at this point is the one that has to do with all those scattered magazines. Fine. You're clear about where you want to make your dent.

For larger projects, after identifying your storage problem in general, you'll probably find it helpful to get more specific. Maybe it's not that your *entire* kitchen is cluttered, for example. When you take a good look at what trips you up every time you attempt to cook a meal, you may see that the real culprits are jumbled drawers that make it impossible to find a ladle or a whisk when you need it and cabinets bursting with plastic ware.

The more specific you can be about your storage needs, the less overwhelming meeting them will seem—and the better prepared you'll be to move on to the next four steps.

# categorize

This is the stage of strategic sorting, of getting even more specific about what you need to store so you can come up with workable solutions.

Let's stick with the kitchen example. If you dump out that drawer of tangled cooking utensils, you'll probably find that you've actually got several categories of items rather than a mass of utensils that are all alike. You might look at them and see that there are several you use almost every day, such as spoons, spatulas, and salad tongs, and others—maybe the meat thermometer and the citrus zester—that you pull out only a few times a year. Your utensils probably also naturally sort themselves into groups according to size or shape (bottle openers and measuring spoons versus the cheese grater and knife sharpener). Or, depending on the size of your collection and on how you cook, it may make sense to you to categorize your utensils by function.

It's not critical that you make final decisions at this point about how you'll ultimately group your cooking utensils or whatever else you're sorting. The objective is simply to break your storage problem down into smaller sets of similar objects so you can begin to get a handle on what you need to store and how.

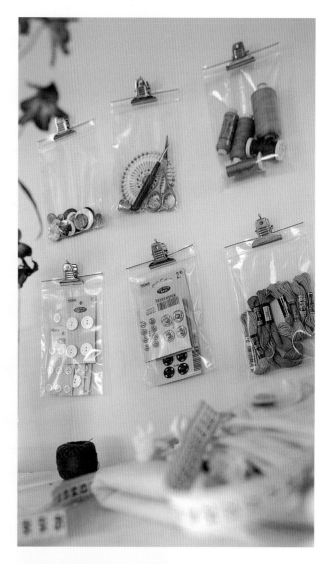

**TOP AND RIGHT:** Once you've sorted what you need to store, it'll be easier to decide which container will do the best job.

## condense

This is where people hit a roadblock. They're afraid condensing means a major (not to mention painstaking) housecleaning initiative aimed at tossing out at least half of the clutter they've carefully accumulated and become attached to over the years.

If you've got the time and patience for a clean sweep, there's no denying it would help reduce your storage needs immensely. But if, like most people, you'd rather ease your way into this, there's a much less intimidating approach. Simply allow condensing to be a natural outgrowth of the categorizing step. It's as painless as looking at those sorted cooking utensils, admitting that you don't *really* need four slotted spoons, and moving two or three of them into the rummage sale pile. Then do the same with the extra sets of measuring cups, the spare soup ladle you've never used, and so on. As you see your stacks shrinking, you just might decide that this condensing business is not only habit-forming, but a whole lot more fun than you thought it would be.

### 10 THINGS MOST PEOPLE HAVE AND CAN PROBABLY LIVE WITHOUT

- Outdated phone books
- Carryout menus from restaurants that have closed
- Expired medicines
- Games your family never plays (and/or games with missing pieces)
- Crushed or torn wrapping paper and ribbons
- Cans of dried-out paint
- Clothing that no longer fits
- Half-used and abandoned bottles of shampoo, lotion, and other toiletries
- Expired coupons
- Old catalogs
- Duplicates of anything, from blow-dryers to blenders

**TOP AND LEFT:** Pare down what you need to store, and you'll be better able to make use of clever container options.

# clarify

Here you get to the heart of tailoring storage solutions to your own specific situation, style, and needs. It's simply a matter of taking the time before you store to clarify the nature of the items to be stored and of your own habits and preferences when it comes to using them.

## clarifying storage items

Once you've got your storage problem sorted into logical groups of items, you get a clearer picture of which ones you want to store within easy reach, which you don't mind using a step stool to get to, which you'd like to store out in the open on display, which you want wrapped in tissue paper and boxed, and so on.

It's at this point, as you assign a kind of hierarchy to your items, that you'll likely want to refine the categories you established earlier. Maybe you divided the cooking utensils, for example, into two categories: one of large utensils and another of small ones. Looking at them now, however, you decide it makes sense to store your five most-often-used utensils all together in one accessible place, regardless of their size. No problem; go ahead and create a third category of frequently used utensils.

## clarifying your habits & preferences

Here's where you inject a critical dose of reality into all the sorting and thinking you've done so far. This step isn't about changing your natural tendencies, but about owning up to them and incorporating them into storage solutions that suit how you live. Here's an example of how.

Say every single evening, without fail, you walk through the door and pile the day's mail on the kitchen counter (makes sense, since the kitchen is where you head first when you get home, to check phone messages and grab something out of the refrigerator). Although you have good intentions of moving it somewhere else later, there the mail stays, taking up a precious chunk of your limited kitchen counter space, until you get around to sorting and responding to it (which you typically do at the nearby kitchen table).

If this is your pattern, one of the worst possible ways to attempt to solve your mail-storage problem would be to put a slotted mail organizer on the tiny table in your bedroom, where you keep telling yourself you *should* sort your mail and pay your bills. Within days, you'll be back to dumping all your envelopes and catalogs where it makes more sense for you to dump them: the kitchen counter. Forget *shoulds* and devise a solution that truly meets your needs—in this case, maybe a mail basket hung from a hook in the corner of the kitchen.

### QUICK QUESTIONS FOR CLARIFYING YOUR STORAGE NEEDS

- Where do I typically use this item?
- When and how often do I use this item?
- Do I want this item stored with or near similar items I often use with it?
- How essential is it that I have easy access to this item?
- What is problematic about where I currently keep this item?
- Even if my current storage system for this item isn't ideal, are there aspects about it that are appealing?

Some items are fine stored in out-of-the-way bins. Others you want to hang close at hand.

# contain

When you think about all the alluring options for containing, from crates, baskets, trunks, and cupboards to bags, racks, and bins, it's so tempting to skip over everything else and jump right to this final step. But the truth is, your job will be much easier if you don't. If you first categorize, condense, and clarify what it is you want to contain, figuring out exactly how to do so will feel like a logical next move rather than an overwhelming undertaking. In addition, working through the steps that lead to this final one will help save you from a common trap: creating more clutter with a bunch of containers that look good but do little to meet your actual needs.

As you'll see in examples throughout the book, containing something can mean far more than boxing it up. When the goal is to rein in the spread of your household's belongings, containing can take the form of everything from hanging keys on labeled hooks to dividing laundry into color-coded bags. Following are the standard storage approaches to consider when it's finally time to put everything in its place.

## hidden storage

Hidden storage is for when you really want to stow something away—preferably behind a closed door or drawer—to mask it from view and/or to protect it from damage. Examples range from plastic, sealable bins full of photo albums in the attic and a caddy of toiletries on the inside of the bathroom cabinet door to specially designed pull-out cabinet inserts and roll-out shelves. Nothing works better than hidden storage if you want to completely eliminate clutter. Just keep in mind that it can require a bit more effort to retrieve items stashed entirely out of sight.

Trunks, baskets, and file boxes are all options for hidden storage.

## display storage

A well-organized storage system can actually double as a decorative feature, whether you hang your hat collection from a series of pegs in the entryway or keep towels in a row of brightly colored straw baskets on a low shelf in the bathroom. Keep your approach simple, and you'll be able to eliminate the chaos while still leaving items out in the open.

## built-in storage

Built-in storage is typically something you're either blessed with or not. Sure, you can add walk-in closets, window seats with lids, and other built-in reconfigurations of your living space, but such solutions are typically beyond the scope of quick and easy do-it-yourself fixes (they're also beyond the scope of this book). What you can do easily is make sure you're taking maximum advantage of the built-ins you've got. Consider options such as adding under-shelf attachable baskets to shelves, equipping closets with pegs and ledges, adding small freestanding storage units such as wine racks and drinking glass containers to the tops of built-in cupboards, and so on.

## freestanding storage

The main advantage of freestanding storage is that it's portable and therefore adaptable. Bookcases, carts, metal shelving units, and furniture pieces such as tables and sideboards equipped with drawers or doors all fall into this category. For even more flexibility, opt for freestanding storage pieces that feature adjustable components (such as shelves you can move to meet your needs) and that are outfitted with wheels, so that rolling the piece here and there (and out of the way) is a no-fuss job.

**TOP**: Display storage

**CENTER**: Adding to built-in storage

**BOTTOM**: Freestanding storage

## item-specific storage

Often purchased pieces, these storage solutions are specially designed to perform specific functions, such as organize your CD collection or keep all the shampoo and soap in one place in the shower. Sometimes an item-specific storage piece is all you need to quickly solve a straightforward storage problem.

## compartmentalized storage

Many times, simply keeping items separated is the key to storing them neatly and efficiently. A drawer divided into distinct sections of rubber bands, paper clips, thumbtacks, and staples, for example, is easier to navigate than one full of a nondescript mass of office supplies. Anything that helps segregate pieces into those helpful, partitioned sections can be thought of as compartmentalized storage, from baskets, jars, and bags to hooks and pegs.

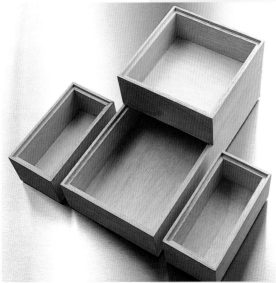

## storage that serves another purpose

Luggage that stores off-season clothing when you're not traveling, a trunk that serves as both a coffee table and a container for photo albums, and vintage hatboxes that house sewing supplies and, at the same time, add a decorative touch to the guest room are all examples of storage that serves another purpose. If you're focused on doing away with clutter, these dual-purpose options can cut your mess in half.

CONTAINER TIP: If every bit of space is precious, don't waste any of it housing oversized storage containers. Match the size of your container to the thing to be contained.

TOP: Item-specific storage
CENTER: Compartmentalized storage
BOTTOM: Storage that serves another purpose

# take stock of what you've got

BEFORE YOU SET OUT ON A SHOPPING SPREE FOR NEW CONTAINERS, TAKE AN INVENTORY OF EXISTING options you may have overlooked. If you're like most people, you've got underutilized spaces and containers that are storage solutions in the making. A piece of pegboard and some hooks, for example, could turn the inside of the door that hides the hot water heater into the perfect holding place for cleaning rags, a broom, a dustpan, and a folding step stool. And maybe you don't need brand new containers for the collection of socks that seems to have outgrown your dresser drawer. Some drawer partitions might be all you need to make your existing space work.

# shelving
# basics

SPEND MORE THAN A FEW MINUTES THINKING ABOUT WHERE YOU'RE GOING TO PUT EVERYTHING YOU'VE PLEDGED TO STORE MORE EFFECTIVELY, and you'll reach the conclusion that flat, horizontal pieces of material mounted strategically around your home are a big part of the answer. Shelves are a hardworking storage staple. They take the form of everything from single ledges to compartmentalized standing units, and they're good for storing such diverse items as spices, gardening supplies, stacks of dishes, and folded sweaters.

You can purchase ready-to-use shelving in a wide variety of styles. Fortunately, with some basic tools and do-it-yourself skills, you can also create and customize your own shelves, whether you want to start from scratch or purchase the components and put them together yourself. On the following pages, we give you step-by-step instructions for making some of the most useful styles of standard shelves.

# making standard shelves

The dimensions and shapes of the shelves in this chapter are simply a starting point. Feel free to adapt them to meet your needs. The only real rule is that it's best to keep the height of the brackets slightly longer than the depth to help distribute your shelf's load. You can also use a range of materials, depending on the look you want and how you plan to finish your shelf. If you're going to paint it, paint-grade lumber or medium density fiberboard (MDF) will work. For a shelf that's purely utilitarian, a good grade of plywood will do. Use hardwoods if you want a natural-wood finish or stained shelves.

## MATERIALS & TOOLS FOR SHELVES

- Sandpaper or rasp
- 8d finish nails
- Wood glue
- Wood filler
- Measuring tools
- Jigsaw
- Hammer
- Nail set

# buying brackets

If you want to skip the step of making your own shelf brackets, manufactured wooden brackets in designs similar to most of those shown in this chapter are available at home centers. You can also buy a variety of metal shelf supports, including versions that you insert into *standards*, slotted metal mounts that attach to the wall and make your shelving adjustable.

## CUT LIST

| DESCRIPTION | QUANTITY | THICKNESS | WIDTH | LENGTH |
|---|---|---|---|---|
| Shelf bracket | 2 | ¾" | 6½" | 8½" |
| Shelf | 1 | ¾" | 8" | 24" |
| Shelf back | 1 | ¾" | 7" | 18½" |

For metric equivalents, see the chart on page 143.

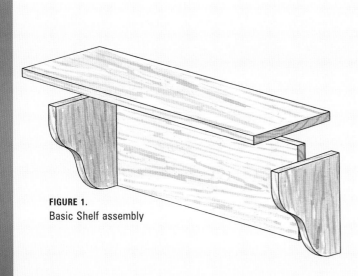

**FIGURE 1.**
Basic Shelf assembly

## basic shelf

### INSTRUCTIONS

1. Mark all your pieces and cut them to size. To mark your brackets, enlarge one of the patterns from page 140 to the size you need, and trace it. Cut the profile with the jigsaw.

2. Smooth the edges of the brackets and the front and side edges of the shelf with sandpaper or a rasp. Leave the back edge of the shelf and the top edges of the shelf back unsanded; they need to be square so they'll fit together accurately. Finish sand both sides of the brackets, the top of the shelf, and the front of the shelf back.

3. Fasten the brackets to the ends of the shelf back. Apply a small amount of wood glue first, then use three or four nails on each end, setting them slightly below the surface. Be sure to align the top and rear edges of each bracket with the top and rear of the shelf back.

4. Nail the shelf to the back and brackets, again using glue first and setting the nails below the surface.

5. Fill the nail holes with wood filler, give the assembled shelf a final sanding, and finish it however you like.

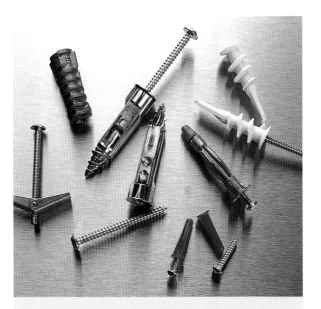

## hanging shelves

How you secure a shelf to a wall depends on what type of wall you've got. If you're working with a hollow, wood-frame wall, the easiest approach is to drive support screws through the shelf and the plaster or drywall and into a wall-framing member, such as a stud, header, or plate. Make sure that at least half the screw's length extends into the framing member. If you're mounting your shelf to a hollow part of the wall (where there's no framing member to screw into), you need to first drill holes in the wall and insert anchors. They'll help hold your screws or bolts in place.

If you're working on solid masonry walls, the screws or bolts you use to hang your shelves need to work in conjunction with some sort of anchor that expands and grips inside the wall. Lead anchors and expansion shields are both standard choices.

A basic home improvement book will provide you with an illustrated chart of wall fasteners and tell you what sort of wall and shelf weight each is best suited for. The folks at your local hardware store can also help guide you toward the right fastener for the job.

## VARIATION 1:
# adding a towel bar

Before assembling the shelf, drill two ¾-inch holes ⅜ inch deep in the two end brackets. Position the holes 2 inches from the back edge of the brackets and 1½ inches from the bottom, and be sure you drill in opposite sides of each bracket, creating mirror-image pieces. Insert a ¾-inch hardwood dowel into the holes, then assemble the shelf. For adding a towel bar to the Basic Shelf (previous page), you'll need a rod that's 19¼ inches long.

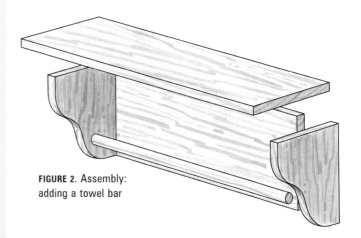

**FIGURE 2.** Assembly: adding a towel bar

## VARIATION 2:
# adding pegs

Cut a scrap piece of lumber the size of your shelf back. Divide it by the number of pegs you want to install plus one. (For example, if you're adding four pegs divide the length by five.) Drill holes the size of the ends of your purchased pegs in the scrap. Temporarily insert the pegs and test the spacing. Once you're satisfied, transfer spacing marks to your shelf back, positioning each hole about 1 inch up from the bottom edge. Add a small amount of glue to the holes, then insert the pegs.

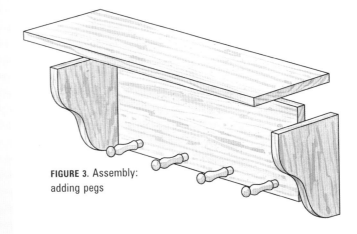

**FIGURE 3.** Assembly: adding pegs

# adding a lower shelf

Cut an additional board measuring 3 x 18½ inches. Sand the top, the bottom, and the front edge, but leave both ends and the back edges square. Measure up 2¾ inches from the bottom of the brackets. Using a square, lightly draw a line on each bracket that's perpendicular to the rear edge of the bracket. You'll use the lines to align the bottom edge of the shelf with the brackets while nailing. Use a couple of nails in each end and across the back to fasten the lower shelf in place.

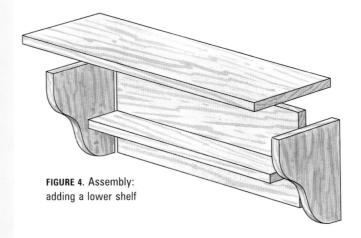

**FIGURE 4.** Assembly: adding a lower shelf

## VARIATION 4:
# adding pigeonholes

Add the lower shelf in Variation 3, then measure the opening between your lower shelf and the top one to determine the height of your pigeonhole dividers. The length of the dividers should match the depth of the lower shelf. Cut the number of dividers you want, and experiment with their placement until you're satisfied. Using a square, mark guidelines where each divider will go, making the lines perpendicular to the front edge of the lower shelf. Sand the dividers, position them, then drive a couple of nails through the top and bottom shelves to fasten them in place.

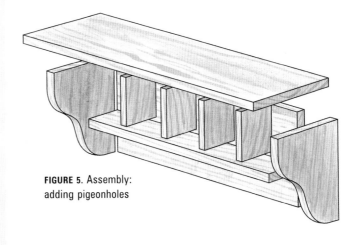

**FIGURE 5**. Assembly: adding pigeonholes

# basic ledge

**INSTRUCTIONS**

1. Mark all your pieces and cut them to size using a jigsaw or a scroll saw. If you want a half-oval ledge, like the one shown here, use a compass to create the shape. To mark your bracket, enlarge the Basic Ledge Bracket pattern, page 140, to the size you need, and trace it.

2. Sand and assemble the pieces, centering the bracket on the shelf back, then following the same process described for assembling the Basic Shelf. Use figure 1 as a guide.

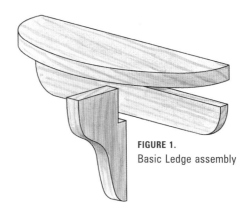

**FIGURE 1.**
Basic Ledge assembly

**CUT LIST**

| DESCRIPTION | QUANTITY | THICKNESS | WIDTH | LENGTH |
|---|---|---|---|---|
| Shelf bracket | 1 | ¾" | 3" | 5" |
| Shelf | 1 | ¾" | 4" | 12" |
| Shelf back | 1 | ½" | 1½" | 12" |

For metric equivalents, see the chart on page 143.

# basic bin shelf

This is simply a flipped-over version of the Basic Shelf, with an added front piece.

## INSTRUCTIONS

1. Mark all your pieces and cut them to size using a jigsaw or a scroll saw. To mark your brackets, enlarge the Bin Shelf Bracket pattern, page 141, to the size you need, and trace it.

2. Sand and assemble the pieces, following the same process described for the Basic Shelf, using figure 1 as a guide.

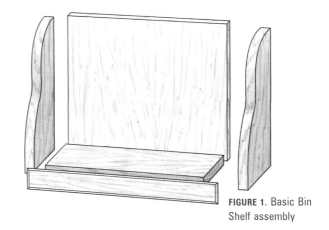

**FIGURE 1.** Basic Bin Shelf assembly

### CUT LIST

| DESCRIPTION | QUANTITY | THICKNESS | WIDTH | LENGTH |
|---|---|---|---|---|
| Shelf brackets | 2 | ¾" | 5¾" | 9¼" |
| Shelf bottom | 1 | ¾" | 5" | 12¾" |
| Shelf back | 1 | ¾" | 9¼" | 12¾" |
| Shelf front | 1 | ¼" plywood | 1½" | 14¾" |

For metric equivalents, see the chart on page 143.

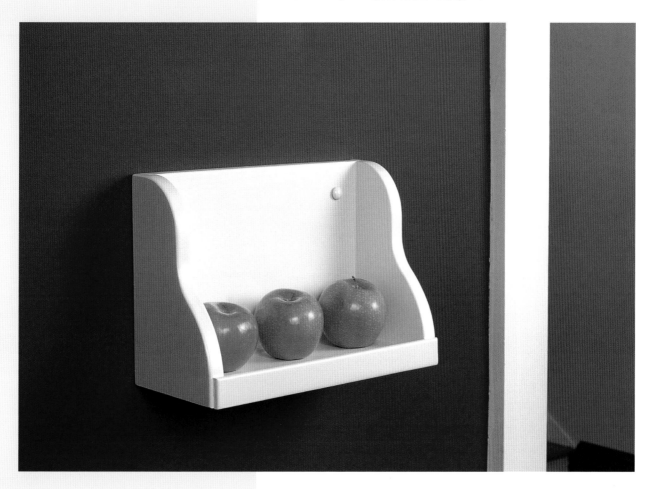

# basic cube

These simple boxes make versatile storage shelves. They also form the basis for other box-style storage units throughout the book.

## CUT LIST

| DESCRIPTION | QUANTITY | THICKNESS | WIDTH | LENGTH |
|---|---|---|---|---|
| Sides | 2 | ½" | 3" | 11" |
| Top & Bottom | 2 | ½" | 3" | 12" |
| Back | 1 | ¼" plywood | 12" | 12" |

For metric equivalents, see the chart on page 143.

## INSTRUCTIONS

1. Cut your pieces to size.

2. Assemble the cube by brushing a little wood glue onto the edges of the pieces, then nailing the top and bottom to the sides. Check to make sure your cube is square, then apply a small amount of glue to the edges of the back piece and nail it in place, using ⅝-inch wire nails or brads.

3. Ease all the edges of the cube with sandpaper.

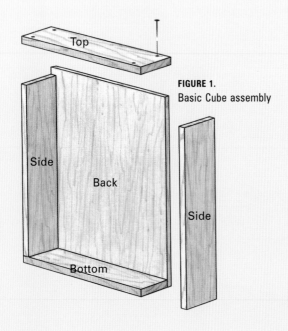

**FIGURE 1.**
Basic Cube assembly

# cube with shelves

You'll need two more pieces of ½-inch board, each 3 inches wide by 11 inches long, to add shelves.

1. Assemble the cube, following the Basic Cube instructions.

2. Before adding the back, slide the shelves into place and nail though the sides to attach them.

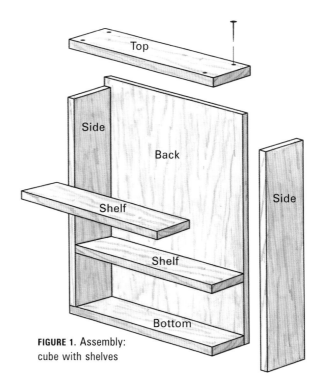

**FIGURE 1.** Assembly: cube with shelves

# cube with pigeonholes

You'll need four more pieces of ½-inch board, each 3 inches wide by 11 inches long, to add pigeonholes.

1. With the jigsaw, cut two notches ½ inch wide by 1⅜ inches deep in each of the four pigeonhole pieces. (If your pigeonhole pieces have designated fronts and backs, be sure to cut two with the notches on the front edge and two with the notches on the back.) Assemble the pigeonhole pieces.

2. Assemble the cube, following the Basic Cube instructions, but before adding the back, slide the assembled pigeonhole pieces into place and nail though the sides to attach them.

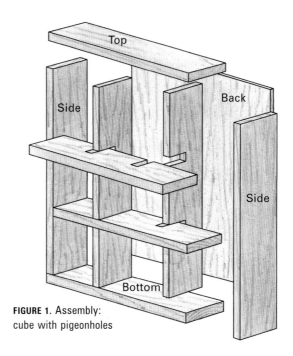

**FIGURE 1.** Assembly: cube with pigeonholes

# living areas

FROM FAMILY ROOMS AND DENS TO
READING NOOKS AND LIVING ROOMS,
these are the heavy-use spaces where we
relax, play, and entertain—not to mention
occasionally work, snack, or grab a nap.
Often, storage solutions and decorating
approaches are one and the same in these
rooms that reflect who we are and how we
live (think of family photos grouped on picture ledges or travel souvenirs arranged on
display shelves). In other cases, you need
storage options that help hide some of the
messier signs of life from view. Either way,
living areas call for practical storage solutions that are also comfortable and personal—and flexible enough to meet the
varied needs of these multipurpose places.

## storage incognito

If you're dealing with limited space and an overabundance of stuff in your living area (and who isn't), few storage solutions are as handy as those that disguise themselves—and do double duty—as something else. Create a coffee table, for example, out of an arrangement of colored metal file boxes (like those on page 32) or a couple of contemporary-looking lidded bins (above), and you've got a flat surface for drinks, candles, or plates of hors d'oeuvres on top. But you've also got a hollow space hidden below for stowing away seldom-used items such as extra winter blankets, old family photo albums, or carefully wrapped china that you pull out only once a year. If sleek and modern isn't exactly your style, put a vintage spin on the same idea by using antique trunks or a series of stacked dish crates (right).

## camouflaged containers

To the right is a starter list of other storage containers that can successfully masquerade as coffee tables, end tables, television and sound-system stands, and other living-area furniture.

- Lidded wicker baskets
- Wooden wine cases
- Barrels
- Wall-mount kitchen cabinets (unmounted, of course)
- Stacked sets of suitcases
- Large aluminum tool chests (the kind designed to fit in the back of pickup trucks)
- Displaced wooden drawers fitted into plywood boxes

# side satchel

Let's get one thing straight. It is not your fault that the novel, the eyeglasses, the reports you bring home from work, the red pen, the highlighter, and the television remote control all eventually end up scattered across various surfaces within arm's reach of your favorite chair. If you had one perfectly designed and unavoidably convenient place to put them all, you would, of course, do so.

## SIDE SATCHEL step-by-step

### MATERIALS & TOOLS

- 1½ yards (1.35 m) of fabric
- Thread (including heavy-duty quilting thread if you're using leather buckles)
- Purchased buckles or closures
- Standard measuring and marking tools
- Sewing machine
- Needles (including size 90/14 if you're using leather buckles)

### CUTTING

CUT THE FOLLOWING PIECES:

- 2 body pieces, each 34 x 17 inches (86.4 x 43.2 cm)
- 2 flaps (Create a flap shape that measures 13 inches [33 cm] on the straight side and curves on the other. Use a standard dinner plate to mark the curve.)
- 2 front pieces, each 13 x 13 inches (33 x 33 cm)
- 4 sides, using the pattern on page 141

### BODY

1. Sew the two body pieces together, right sides together, using a ½-inch (1.3 cm) seam allowance and leaving a 4 to-5-inch (10.2 to 12.7 cm) opening for turning.

2. Press the seams to set the stitching, turn the body right side out, and press the seams again.

3. Turn the raw edges of the opening inside, and stitch it closed.

4. Topstitch around sides, 1 inch (2.5 cm) from the edges, for stability.

### POCKET

You'll sew one actual pocket and another that you'll use for the pocket lining. Use a contrasting fabric for the lining, if you like.

1. Place the right sides of one front piece and two side pieces together. Sew the side pieces in place, using a ½-inch (1.3 cm) seam allowance. Repeat for the lining pieces.

2. Press the seams, then trim them.

3. Sew the two pieces from step 1 together, right sides together, using a ½-inch (1.3 cm) seam allowance and leaving a 4 to 5-inch (10.2 to 12.7 cm) opening for turning.

4. Press the seams and turn the pocket right side out.

5. Turn the raw edges of the opening inside, and stitch it closed.

6. If you want to create a "tuck" look (like the one on the satchel shown), fold along the seam where you joined the front pieces to the sides, and stitch ⅜ inch (9.5 mm) in from the edge.

## FLAP

1. Sew the two flap pieces, right sides together, using a ½-inch (1.3 cm) seam allowance and leaving a 3 to 4-inch (7.6 to 10.2 cm) opening on the straight edge for turning.

2. Press the seams, clip the curved seam, and turn the flap right side out.

3. Press the raw edges of the opening inside. You'll close them when you attach the flap to the body.

## ASSEMBLY

1. Position the flap over the pocket to determine placement for the buckles. Mark the placement. Sew the buckle portion with the hole section on the flap and the other portion on the pocket. Reinforce the stitching by sewing in an "X" pattern.

2. Position the pocket on the body, 2 inches (5.1 cm) from the bottom and from both sides. Sew the pocket in place, sewing close around the three edges and using a multistitch for strength. Note: There will be a pleat at each bottom corner. Ease in the excess fabric; this creates depth in the pocket.

3. Center the flap over the pocket. Sew it in place along the straight edge, stitching close to the edge of the flap. Reinforce the flap with a second set of stitches ⅜ inch (9.5 mm) from your original line.

# it's the little things

**problem:**

Storing buttons, thread, needles, and other miscellaneous mending supplies

**solution:**

Sort your supplies, put the sorted groups into sealable plastic bags, clamp the bags with binder clips (the kind you can find in any office supply store), and hang the clips from nails or hooks. Your nails or hooks can be out in the open (maybe on a bulletin board in a corner) or concealed on the inside of a cabinet door. This is also a good solution for storing jewelry, hair accessories, or home office supplies such as paper clips, thumbtacks, and rubber bands.

## storage to go

Equip a storage piece with wheels so it can easily roll from here to there, and a fixture that was once set in its ways suddenly becomes a versatile problem solver that's happy to change location to meet your changing needs. Baskets and bins that have been outfitted with casters allow you to wheel a supply of crossword puzzles or letter-writing materials right up next to your chair and then out of the way when you're finished. Small tables and benches on wheels make it possible to roll televisions and sound systems from spot to spot—or completely out of sight. And low platforms on rollers can slide effortlessly under couches or chairs to serve as hidden storage. A large storage piece like the one shown here could even be rolled into another room and transformed into a table extension for a holiday dinner.

### adding casters

To make your storage go places, simply attach small wheels on swivels that support moveable weight. Casters are categorized according to how heavy a load they can handle (100-pound [45 kg] load-bearing casters, for example). They also come in two primary styles: one with fixture plates that you screw in place and the other with stems you insert in drilled holes. Screw-in-place casters work best on pieces that feature a flat base area, such as a platform or a wastebasket. If you're adding casters to individual furniture legs, stem-type casters provide sturdier support.

# salvage solutions

HERE'S AN IDEA THAT'S A CLASSY STEP UP FROM THAT DORM-ROOM storage staple: the plastic milk crate. This wooden shipping crate, perked up with a splash of white paint, flipped on its side, and fitted with wheels, becomes an end table, serving cart, and portable bookshelf in one. Auctions, flea markets, and summer produce stands are great places to shop for similar-looking wooden crates.

# reading caddy
# with canvas sleeves

Say you've got one member of the household who simply must keep up with the latest fashions, another who loves to cook, and a third who's a news junkie. That could translate into at least half a dozen magazines showing up in your mailbox each month—and quickly making their way to tables, couches, the floor, and other surface spaces where they're stacked and saved for future reading. Imagine how much happier you'd be if you could sort all that must-have reading material into neat little canvas sleeves, and slide it all out of the way (maybe even under a nearby table) for the 23 hours a day no one's using it.

# reading caddy step-by-step

## CUT LIST

| DESCRIPTION | QUANTITY | THICKNESS | WIDTH | LENGTH |
|---|---|---|---|---|
| Sides | 4 | 2" | 2" | 16¼" |
| Legs | 4 | 2" | 2" | 16" |

For metric equivalents, see the chart on page 143.

## MATERIALS & TOOLS

- Sandpaper
- Wood glue
- Wood filler
- 1¾-inch brads, 18 gauge
- 1 set of ⅝-inch stem-type casters
- 12 dowel rods, ⅜ x 13⅞ inches
- Rope for handles
- Measuring tools
- Table saw
- Thickness planer
- Router
- Drill and appropriately sized bits
- Hammer
- Nail set
- Clamps

## INSTRUCTIONS

The most difficult part of building this caddy will be locating a source for 2-inch thick lumber. Start at a woodworking store or lumberyard that specializes in hardwoods. Mail-order sources are also an option. As a last resort, make your own material by gluing three pieces of ¾-inch lumber together and resizing. You'll also need to cut mortise and tenon joints to make this piece. If you're unfamiliar with the techniques for doing so, a basic woodworking book can show you how.

1. Using the table saw and thickness planer, dimension all your material to 2 inches square. The exact final dimension is not as important as being certain that all your material is square and the same size. Cut all your pieces to length.

2. Working with the side pieces, use figure 1 as a guide to lay out and cut tenons 1⅛ inches long by ½ inch wide. Center the tenons on both ends of each side piece. Trim ½ inch off the top of each tenon and cut a 45° angle.

3. Using a tenon as a guide, lay out and cut mortises ½ inch wide and 1⅛ inch deep in two adjacent faces of each leg. These mortises will intersect at right angles. The 45° angle you cut on the ends of the tenons provides for clearance at the intersection. See figure 2 for a view of mortise placement.

4. Using your router, cut a ledge ½ x ½ inch along the inside edge of two of the side pieces. On the other two side pieces, drill two holes approximately 4 inches apart, centered on both the length and width. The size of the holes should accommodate the rope you've chosen for handles.

5. On the bottom of each leg, drill centered holes to accommodate your casters.

6. On the sidepieces with ledges, apply wood glue to all surfaces of the tenons and to one mortise of each leg. Be sure to select mortises that are mirror images of each other. Assemble and clamp the joints. Check to be certain the legs and sides are square to each other, and adjust them if necessary.

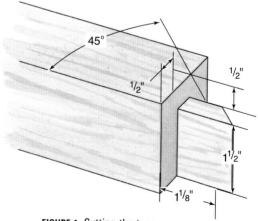

**FIGURE 1.** Cutting the tenons

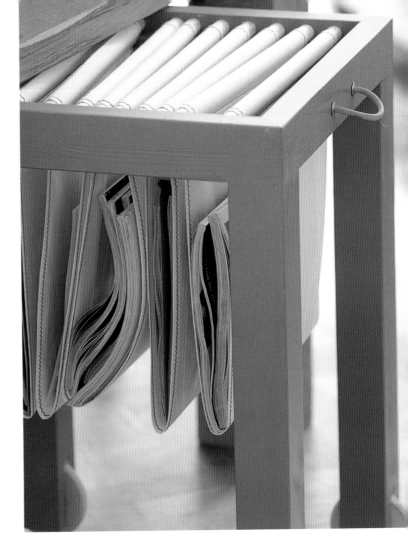

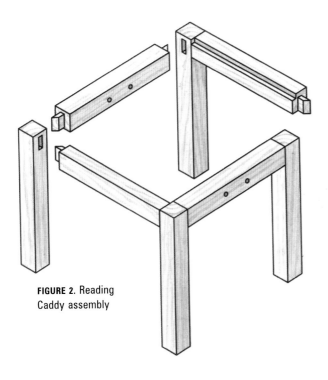

**FIGURE 2.** Reading Caddy assembly

7. On the inside faces of the legs, pin the tenons in the mortises, using a couple of brad nails. Be certain to check that everything is square before pinning the tenons in place. Clamp the assemblies together and let them set for an hour. Finish the assembly by gluing and clamping the remaining two sides. Again, see figure 2. Let the final assembly set for an hour.

8. Measure the actual distance between the edges of the ledges on the final assembly. Subtract ⅛ inch for clearance, and cut the dowel rods to length.

9. Sand the entire assembly, easing all the square edges, and finish your caddy any way you like.

10. Add the casters, the rope handles, and the canvas sleeves. Secure the handles with an overhand knot on the inside of the caddy. A small amount of wood glue on the knots will keep them from coming undone.

## creating the canvas sleeves

### MATERIALS & TOOLS

- 2 yards (1.8 m) canvas
- Contrasting thread
- Scissors
- Ruler
- Sewing machine

### INSTRUCTIONS

1. Measure and cut out six lengths of canvas, each 24 inches (61 cm) long and 13 inches (33 cm) wide.

2. Fold over a ½-inch (1.3 cm) hem on each long side. Stitch each hem with a decorative zigzag stitch. Repeat for each length of fabric.

3. Fold over a 1-inch (2.5 cm) hem on each short side. Stitch the hem with a zigzag stitch. Repeat for each length of fabric.

4. Thread a dowel rod through the 1-inch (2.5 cm) hem on each length of fabric. Fold the length of fabric in half and slide the dowel rods into position on the rack.

# Multitaskers

In an age when performing several functions simultaneously has become both necessity and fine art, it's especially satisfying to find furniture that can beautifully handle more than one task at a time. With its broad, flat top that runs the length of the couch, the piece shown here is the sort of living room table everyone could use. It offers surface space on top, like any other table, for flower arrangements, books, reading lamps, and a knickknack or two. But factor in the expansive cubbyhole openings below, and it's also a dream-come-true storage unit that's functional and decorative at the same time. If you want one just like it, here's some great news: it's actually not much more than an expanded version of many of the other basic boxes we show you how to build throughout the book. Here's how to adapt the instructions and make a multitasking storage table of your own.

## cube table step-by-step

### CUT LIST

| DESCRIPTION | QUANTITY | THICKNESS | WIDTH | LENGTH |
|---|---|---|---|---|
| Sides | 2 | ¾" | 16½" | 24" |
| Top & Bottom | 2 | ¾" | 18" | 48" |
| Divider | 1 | ¾" | 16½" | 24" |
| Back | 1 | ¼" plywood | 24" | 48" |
| Base | 4 | ¾" | 4" | 21" |
| Base Locators | 4 | ¾" | 2" | 16" |
| Base Locators | 4 | ¾" | 2" | 14" |
| Base Locators | 4 | ¾" | 2" | 7½" |
| Base Locators | 4 | ¾" | 2" | 5½" |

For metric equivalents, see the chart on page 143.

### MATERIALS & TOOLS

- 8d finish nails
- 1¼-inch wire nails, 18 gauge
- Sandpaper
- Wood glue
- Wood filler
- Measuring tools
- Handsaw or jigsaw
- Hammer
- Nail set

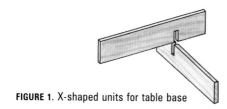

**FIGURE 1.** X-shaped units for table base

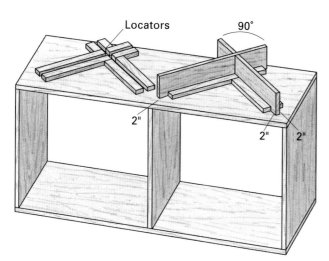

**FIGURE 2.** Placing the locator strips

### INSTRUCTIONS

1. Cut all of your pieces to size.

2. The table base is made up of two X-shaped units constructed with half-lap joinery. To make them, use the handsaw or jigsaw to cut a notch 2 inches deep x ¾ inch wide, 5½ inches from the rear edge on all four base pieces. Assemble the pieces into two X-shaped units (see figure 1).

3. On the bottom of your box, measure and mark lines 2 inches in from the edges of both sides and the front. Using these lines as guides, position the X-shaped units on the bottom of the box. Check the intersections to make sure they're square.

4. Place the locator strips along the edges of the X-shaped units (see figure 2). Fasten them to the bottom of the box using glue and wire nails.

5. Remove the X-shaped units, spread some glue into the locator slots, then reinstall the units, making sure they're completely seated against the bottom of the box. Allow about an hour for the glue to set up before you turn the completed unit over.

6. Set any visible nails slightly below the surface. Fill the resulting holes with wood filler, and give the entire piece a final sanding before finishing it.

**problem:**

Shallow drawers that are often a feature of end tables and other pieces of living-area furniture. They offer an ingenious little out-of-the-way storage opportunity, but tend to fill up with a tangled mess of odds and ends.

**solution:**

Pick up some thin, various-sized balsa trays at craft stores, and use them to create removable sections for sorting what you store in your drawer—maybe pocket change in one, cat toys in another, and pens and notepaper in a third.

it's
the
little
things

# collections

Even the confirmed minimalists among us tend to have something they're so fond of they can't resist amassing lots of it, in all its many variations of color, size, shape, and style. Fortunately, figuring out how to store whatever it is you collect is as easy as deciding how you want to show it off. Whether you're wild about antique baking pans or obsessed with decks of playing cards, your cherished pieces are just the sort of conversation starters that give a home character and personality. Display-style storage, from shelves and ledges to clear glass jars and cabinets with see-through doors, let you store and spotlight your pieces at the same time.

A basic display case like the one shown here is a perfect storage container for a set of miniatures. Simply build the Basic Cube with Shelves, page 31, using custom-cut glass shelves instead of wooden shelves. If you want to add a glass door to the front of your case, use a frame that fits your cube opening, fill it with a piece of glass, hinge it to the top of the cube, and add a latch at the bottom.

## collection storage tips

- Check the weight-bearing capacity of any shelves before loading them up with heavy, breakable collectibles such as ceramic pieces or glass objects.

- If you've got so many pieces your display feels overwhelming, try grouping them into smaller arrangements organized by color, size, or shape.

- Collectibles don't have to simply sit on a surface. Hang your 1950s' diner cups from hooks on the wall, put the beach glass you gathered last summer into Mason jars and set them in the window where the glass will catch the light, and pile all of your childhood dolls and stuffed animals into an antique wagon.

- Assign the status of collection to anything you've got a lot of. If your scarves fill up an entire drawer, pull them out and put them on display on a peg rail in the hallway.

COUNT IT AS ONE OF LIFE'S GREAT MYSTERIES. SOMEHOW, a stack of stuff on the floor is a mess, while the same stuff, separated from the floor by nothing more than the base of a clever container, is not only acceptable but downright appealing. Here, a whitewashed wooden tray and an old wooden grain trough turn extra serving bowls, a sound system, and a pile of news-papers into interesting aspects of the room's decor.

baskets
boxes
&bins

## sideboard storage

Originally developed as dining room serving stations and later popular as office furniture, credenzas like these, with their long, flat tops and spacious storage cavities, are perfect pieces for a home's main living areas. On top, you can blur the lines between storage and decor. Dress the surface with an uncrowded arrangement of pieces from your collection of glass bottles, vintage cocktail shakers, or handmade vases. Or use it as a spot to feature some of your favorite books or photographs. Inside, you've got a luxurious amount of space where you can stash away anything you want within easy reach but out of sight. You get at what's inside this especially useful sideboard through a series of hinged doors. If it's exactly what you've been looking for, follow the instructions on the next page for making one of your own.

## sideboard storage step-by-step

### MATERIALS & TOOLS

- 1 assembled Cube Table, page 47
- ¾-inch plywood for doors
- Purchased handles
- Full overlay hinges, 2 per door
- Measuring tools
- Circular saw
- Screwdriver

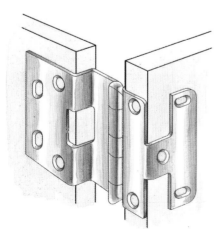

**FIGURE 1.** Full overlay hinges allow you to put fasteners in two surfaces—in this case, the door and the table frame—making the hinge connection especially strong.

### INSTRUCTIONS

FOR METRIC EQUIVALENTS, SEE THE CHART ON PAGE 143.

The Cube Table shown earlier in this chapter (page 47) forms the basis for this sideboard. Adding the X-shaped base units is optional.

1. Cut doors to fit the cube openings, making the edges flush with the top, bottom, and sides of the openings. Leave a ⅛-inch gap between each door.

2. Use full overlay hinges to attach the doors to the table frame, following the hinge manufacturer's instructions and using the hardware packaged with the hinges. You can attach your doors so they open sideways or from top to bottom. If you choose the second option, consider also installing a lightweight chain (available at hardware stores and home centers) to one side of each door for added support.

3. Attach purchased handles to each door.

**DESIGN TIP:** Dress up your sideboard a bit by purchasing custom-made doors at a cabinet shop. Build the sideboard and purchase your hinges first, then take the exact door-opening measurements and your hinges with you when you place your order.

ONE OF THE UPSIDES OF THE LOW-TECH DAYS WHEN OFFICE WORK INVOLVED index cards, steno pads, and honest-to-goodness carbon copies is that there were lots of nifty furniture pieces full of compartments, cubbies, and various-sized drawers designed to organize and store all of the paperwork and related supplies. Today, cabinets, filing units, and other pieces that once supported office systems can help with specialized living-area storage. Keep a lookout, and chances are you'll find a piece that's just right for neatly filing away years' worth of snapshots, dozens of Christmas ornaments, or your alphabetized collection of CDs.

# salvage solutions

# kitchens & dining rooms

SINCE THE DAYS WHEN KITCHENS AND DINING AREAS WERE MERELY OPEN HEARTHS IN ONE-ROOM HOUSES, they've functioned as the center of the home. What's changed, of course, is that today these primary gathering places have to hold many more appliances, gadgets, and specialty accessories than they once did. Now that juicers jockey for shelf space with espresso makers and omelette pans clatter around in cupboards beside 13-quart Dutch ovens, the time has come to impose some order on these bustling household hubs.

## spice drawers

Maybe you actually listened to your mother, and before you start cooking, you assemble a neat, countertop arrangement of every single ingredient the recipe says you'll need. If, on the other hand, you're like most of us, the onions are already sizzling madly in the skillet before you see the note about one teaspoon of ground cardamom and begin wondering whether you have any. Rather than fight your natural approach to food preparation, why not just make sure your spices are ready to step in at the last minute? If they're in clear view and within easy reach (as opposed to stacked behind bottles of flavored vinegar in a dark cabinet above the stove), you can quickly grab a pinch of whatever you need when you need it. Here are two different ways to transform a kitchen drawer into an accessible way to store spices.

## spice drawer #1 step-by-step

1. Start with a supply of small jars that clear the top of your drawer. You can buy jars at kitchen accessory stores or recycle your own; those that hold baby food, pimentos, or artichoke hearts are about the size you'll probably need.

2. Wash and dry your jars thoroughly.

3. Fill each jar with a frequently used spice. Store the jars flipped over for a clean, modern look. If you want to label each, use a metallic paint marker to do so.

## spice drawer #2 step-by-step

1. Purchase small metal (or plastic or wooden) bins that fit down in your drawer.

2. Arrange the bins in tightly packed rows, so they create a compartmentalized drawer.

3. Purchase your spices in bulk, and fill each bin with a different one. This approach works best for spices you use (and use up) regularly, since they won't be protected in air-tight containers. For spices you expect to have on hand for a while, stick with Spice Drawer #1.

# salvage
# solutions

NOW THAT WE CAN MANEUVER OUR WAY THROUGH THE DEWEY DECIMAL SYSTEM using computer keyboards, libraries have little need for those handsome old pieces of furniture known as card catalogs. But the valuable storage chests have by no means outlived their usefulness. Snag one at an auction or antique shop, and you've got a dining area hutch that will store your candles, napkin rings, linens, and good silver all in separate drawers—and serve as a mealtime conversation piece at the same time.

Maybe you need a neat system for packing away the good stuff you pull out and polish only a couple of times a year. Or perhaps your problem is drawer space, and you'd like to find a way to store your everyday forks and knives without resorting to the usual drawer-insert divider. In either case, a hanging organizer with clear pockets—the kind most often used to hold shoes, stockings, or jewelry—can be an innovative solution. Suspend it from the back of a cabinet or closet door, and you've got handy little compartments in which you can tuck everything from butter knives to dessert spoons.

# silver storage

# kitchen air rights

Just ask any big-city real estate developer, sometimes the only direction left to build is up. If extra storage space in your kitchen is as rare as a vacant lot in the middle of a thriving commercial district, there are plenty of ways to move pots, pans, bottles, cookbooks, and long-handled utensils up and out of the way. Best of all, you can actually enhance your kitchen's "skyline" in the process.

Wall-mount stainless steel grids and holders, metal rails that hang from shelves and cabinets, and racks that suspend from ceilings can all give your cooking area the flair of a restaurant kitchen while creating valuable vacancies in its cupboards, cabinets, and drawers. Housewares stores sell a wide variety of mountable options for kitchen storage. They're easy to install and typically made to accommodate removable S hooks, so you can hang your pans, gadgetry, and supplies in any configuration you like. In addition, on page 68 we offer some simple instructions for making your own pot rack out of galvanized plumbing pipe.

**LEFT AND ABOVE:** This wall-mounted system is built from bars and hanging shelves that remove the clutter from counters and cabinets.

**RIGHT:** Easy-to-mount pot racks are available at housewares stores and come with the hardware you need to hang them.

## pipe dreams

Like a great big set of grown-up Tinkertoys, galvanized plumbing pipe comes in modular units you can fit together into all kinds of creative configurations. The result: contemporary, industrial-look frames that are sturdy enough for all kinds of heavy-duty kitchen storage. You'll find the threaded pipe at home improvement stores in standard lengths such as 18, 24, and 30 inches (45.7, 61, and 76.2 cm). Additional pieces, called elbow joints and T-connectors, connect the lengths to each other. Here, we've come up with a couple of easy-to-assemble combinations of pipes and connectors, one for a mobile chopping block table and the other for a hanging pot rack.

## chopping block table step-by-step

This versatile kitchen storage and worktable can be built to any configuration. The tabletop you purchase will dictate the size of the unit. We used an inexpensive pine tabletop measuring 20 x 40 inches (50.8 x 101.6 cm), but you could invest in a custom-sized hardwood butcher-block top for even better durability.

**MATERIALS & TOOLS**

- 1 x 20 x 48 inch (2.5 x 50.8 x 121.9 cm) glued pine board top
- Polyurethane finish (if desired)
- 4 galvanized threaded pipes, 1 x 18 inch (2.5 x 45.7 cm)
- 4 galvanized threaded pipes, 1 x 12 inch (2.5 x 30.5 cm)
- 2 galvanized threaded pipes, 1 x 30 inch (2.5 x 76.2 cm)
- 4 galvanized T-connectors, 1 inch (2.54 cm) diameter
- Cleaning solvent or label remover solvent
- Abrasive pad
- 4 galvanized flanges, 1 inch (2.5 cm) diameter
- #12 x ¾ inch (1.9 cm) wood screws (You'll need 16.)
- 12-inch (30.5 cm) length of 1-inch (2.5 cm) diameter wood dowel (optional)
- 2 galvanized door pulls, 4⅞ inches (12.4 cm) long
- 4 casters (optional)
- Teflon tape
- Pipe wrench
- Ruler
- Pencil
- Electric drill and bits
- Screwdriver
- Handsaw
- Half-round file

1. Finish the tabletop before assembling the table.

2. You'll soon discover that the pipes are coated with some sort of oily substance. Use the cleaning solvent to remove any labels and oily residue. Then, use the abrasive pad to scour the pipes. Set them aside.

3. Wrap a short length of teflon tape on the threaded ends of the 30-inch (76.2 cm) pipes. Attach the center portion of each T-connector to each end of the pipes. Use the pipe wrench to tighten the connection. Check to see that the T-connectors lie flat on the floor without rocking. They must be parallel; adjust them if necessary.

4. Wrap the tape on the threaded ends of the 18-inch (45.7 cm) lengths of pipe. Attach one end of each to one end of each T-connector, and tighten them with the pipe wrench. These pieces form the upper parts of the table legs.

5. Attach a flange to the other ends of the 18-inch (45.7 cm) pipes.

6. Lay the pine tabletop face down on a flat working surface. Set the assembled sections with the flanges on the underside of the tabletop. Center the sections on the top, and mark the points for the screws. Use the drill and appropriate size bit to drill shallow pilot holes in the tabletop.

7. Attach the flanges to the tabletop with the wood screws.

8. Use the handsaw to cut the dowel into four lengths, each 3 inches (7.6 cm) long. Select a bit comparable to the stem of your casters. Drill a hole centered on one end of each dowel length, deep enough to insert a caster. Insert a dowel into one end of each piece of 12-inch (30.5 cm) pipe. You may need to file the interior of the pipe with the half-round file to "de-burr" the interior. If you don't have a file, use coarse sandpaper to reduce the diameter of the dowel to fit inside the pipe. Set the dowels aside.

9. Wrap teflon tape on the other ends of the 12-inch (30.5 cm) pipes, and screw them into the remaining openings on the T-connectors. Tighten them with the pipe wrench. These pieces form the bottom parts of the table legs.

10. Ask someone to help you turn the table right side up. Then, have your helper lift one end, insert a caster into a dowel, and slip it inside one of the legs. Repeat with the other leg and then with both legs on the other end of the table.

11. Attach the door pulls on the front side or end of the table, using the hardware packaged with the pulls. Place storage baskets across the base pipes, if you like.

**VARIATIONS:**

- If you want your table to be stationary, forget the steps for adding casters. Fit rubber caps over the bottom ends of the 12-inch (30.5 cm) pipes, instead.

- For a table with additional base support, replace each of the side rail pipes with two 12-inch (30.5 cm) pipes connected with a T-connector. Connect the side rails to each other with a third piece of pipe that forms a trestle. (The length of the trestle will depend on the size of your table.) See figure 1.

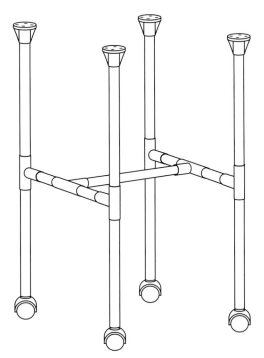

**FIGURE 1.** Adding a trestle for additional base support

# salvage
# solutions

THIS SNAZZY LITTLE PORTABLE BAR, WHICH HOLDS BOTTLES ABOVE, MIXERS below, and napkins, plates, and coasters in the drawer, began life as a cart for surgical tools. Leave it to people whose professional supplies must be organized with absolute precision to come up with the ultimate workplace storage pieces—then find out where they sell them when they upgrade to the newer model!

## pot rack step-by-step

The lengths of pipe and number of connectors and flanges you need will depend on the space you're working with. Other materials and tools for creating and installing your rack are identical to those for creating the Chopping Block Table, page 65.

**INSTRUCTIONS**

1. Locate ceiling joists and wall studs in the area where you want to hang your rack. For stability, you'll want to anchor it into structural supports.

2. Based on your anchor points, determine your rack's design. A simple square is fine. You may also want two levels of hanging bars, like those on the rack shown here. The higher bar is for pots and utensils with long handles. The lower bar makes it easy to reach pieces with short handles.

3. Purchase your pipe and connectors, and clean them (see step 2, page 66).

4. Use teflon tape and a pipe wrench to connect your pieces, according to your design.

5. Attach flanges to the end pieces.

6. Screw the flanges into your ceiling and, if necessary, your wall, making sure the screws are long enough to reach into the joists and/or studs.

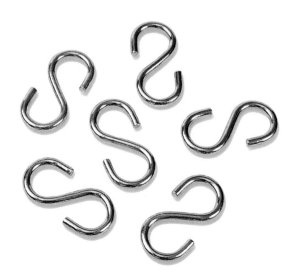

# hardworking furniture

The idea here is not that you've got to have a sideboard exactly like this one in your pantry (or that you've got to have a sideboard or a pantry either one, for that matter). What you do need, though, is an eye for furniture pieces that can help you maximize your storage options. A kitchen worktable that features a lower ledge like this one, for example, gives you twice as much surface area without demanding any more space in the room. One that's equipped with deep drawers like these beneath the work surface is a whole lot more useful than one without. So, though storage potential may not be the first quality that comes to mind when you're picking out a piece of furniture, factor it into the mix, and you'll happily take home more than you bargained for.

# baskets & boxes & bins

IT'S SO SATISFYING WHEN A SINGLE STORAGE SOLUTION TAKES CARE OF A COUPLE OF problems. Say you've got a few great big serving bowls that you use only on the rare occasions when you make mashed potatoes for a crowd or feed chips and salsa to all your friends at once. You've got to do something with them during the rest of the year. Rather than searching in vain for an out-of-the-way spot that's big enough to store them, leave your bowls on display and turn them into storage bins themselves. They're the perfect containers for fresh fruit from the market, vegetables from the garden, and miscellaneous kitchen-and-dining supplies, from candles to packages of cocktail napkins.

## utensils

Toss them all into one big drawer together and close them away, and utensils behave like unruly children who know they'll get attention if they cause a ruckus. The next time you reach in for the pasta tongs, you'll have to break up fights, untangle arguments, and separate the pieces that can't seem to get along. And it will be that way every time. But take your utensils out and dress them up with some imaginative containers, and you'll find they typically rise to the occasion. They'll be much more cooperative when you have to pick one out for a special task, and those waiting their turn will quietly add a bit of gourmet flair to the atmosphere.

The hanging containers shown here, made from metal file boxes, add an unexpected industrial touch to the kitchen wall. Countertop options in other styles range from tin buckets to flea market pitchers.

# hanging utensil box step-by-step

**MATERIALS & TOOLS**

- Metal storage containers (Try office supply stores.)
- Screws (Choose a type appropriate for your wall.)
- Washers
- Electric drill and bits
- Pencil
- Level

**INSTRUCTIONS**

1. Drill two widely spaced holes on the back side of your container. Be sure the bit you use is the right size for your mounting screws.

2. Hold the container where you want it on the wall, check to make sure it's level, then use your pencil and the holes in your container to mark the hanging spots on the wall. Predrill the holes in the wall before you mount the box if you're hanging it on a masonry wall.

3. Use a washer with each screw as you mount the container on the wall.

## mounting a pegboard step-by-step

**MATERIALS & TOOLS**

- Pegboard (A standard sheet is 24 x 48 inches [61 x 122 cm].)

- 6 feet (1.8 m) of pine board, ¾ x 2 inches

- 6 screws (Choose screws appropriate for your mounting surface.)

- 9 flathead screws, ¾ inch (1.9 cm)

- Handsaw

- Ruler

- Pencil

- Electric drill and drill bits

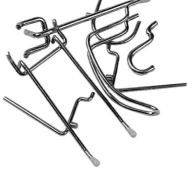

**INSTRUCTIONS**

1. Divide the pine board into three equal, 24-inch (61 cm) sections, marking each. Cut the board with the handsaw along the marked lines to create the cleats on which you'll mount your pegboard.

2. In each cleat, drill a hole 2 inches (5.1 cm) in from each end. Use a drill bit sized to match your mounting screws.

3. Measure and mark the placement of each cleat on your wall, door back, or other surface. You want a cleat at the top, center, and bottom of the pegboard to give it stability and stand it away from the surface.

4. Attach the cleats to the mounting surface.

5. Use the ¾-inch (1.9 cm) flathead screws to attach the pegboard to the cleats.

## pegboard storage

All it takes to turn any vertical surface into the equivalent of an industrial-strength bulletin board is a section of pegboard and a supply of hooks. The board's inviting pattern of evenly spaced holes provides a blank and adaptable canvas for hanging a series of storage baskets, stringing a suspension wire, or simply adding hooks for dish towels and utensils.

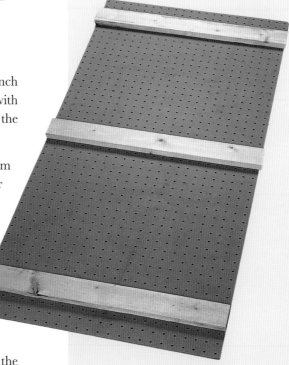

# making sense
# of molding

Who knows why those ornamental strips of wood that separate sections of walls originally came about. What they're useful for in an age of abundance is the display-style storage of anything that looks appealing propped on the little ledge they create (think platters, pictures, mirrors, and the like). No need to despair if your walls are molding free. You can fashion your own customized molding ledge in a flash.

## molding ledge step-by-step

**MATERIALS & TOOLS**

- Brick molding
- 1 x 4 board
- Lengths of backbend molding for ledge lip
- Sandpaper
- Acrylic paint (or other finishing materials)
- Finishing nails
- Wood screws
- Level
- Measuring tools
- Electric drill and bit to fit screws
- Hammer

**INSTRUCTIONS**

1. Finish sand and paint or otherwise finish your molding pieces before hanging them.

2. Use a level to hang your brick molding with finishing nails.

3. Screw the 1 x 4 board (which becomes your ledge) on top of the brick molding (see figure 1).

4. Use small finishing nails to attach the lip piece to the ledge.

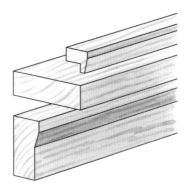

**FIGURE 1.** Molding ledge assembly

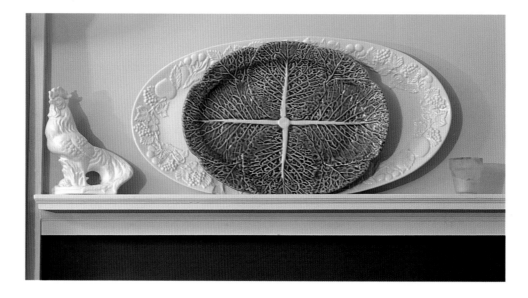

# vertical retrofitting

Kitchenware stores sell vertical cabinet dividers made of either wood or plastic and designed as solid panels or sets of divider dowels. They can help you keep everything from muffin tins to cookie sheets in clear view but separate, so one can be removed without disturbing any of the others. If you'd rather customize your cabinet dividers, follow the instructions here for building a basic box with a series of dowel rods that will slide into a cabinet or onto a shelf.

# cabinet divider step-by-step

## MATERIALS & TOOLS

- Wood to build a box (Dimensions will depend on the size box you're building.)
- Dowel rods
- 8d finish nails
- Sandpaper
- Wood glue
- Wood filler
- Measuring tools
- Circular saw
- Drill and drill bits to match your dowel size
- Hammer
- Nail set

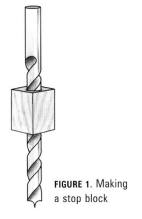

FIGURE 1. Making a stop block

## INSTRUCTIONS

FOR METRIC EQUIVALENTS, SEE THE CHART ON PAGE 143.

1. Following the instructions on page 30 for the Basic Cube, measure and cut pieces for a box sized to fit your space.

2. Determine the diameter and even spacing of your dowel rods, then mark the centers of the holes you'll need for those rods near the front and back of your box's bottom piece. Don't forget to allow for the diameter of the dowels when you're calculating the openings in between them. Also, remember to account for the thickness of the side pieces, which will fit on the inside of the bottom piece. Mark matching dowel holes on the box's top piece.

3. Use a hand drill to drill the holes approximately ½ inch deep, being careful to drill at an exact right angle. To make sure your holes will all be the same depth, make a stop block out of a scrap of wood (see figure 1). Slip the block over your drill bit, then mount the bit in your drill chuck so the amount of bit exposed matches the depth of the holes you want. If you're planning to do a lot of drilling, a basic woodworking book can also give you information on building a drill jig (a template that helps with accurate hole placement) and on using a drill press (which helps insure that your holes are square).

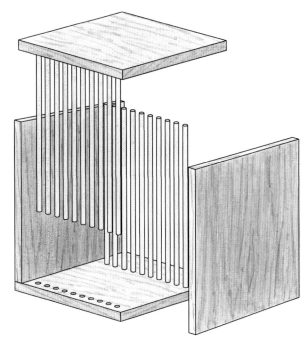

FIGURE 2. Cabinet Divider assembly

4. Cut the number of dowels you need to length, which should be 1⁄16 inch *less* than the height of the opening between the box's top and bottom *plus* twice the hole depth.

5. Attach the sides to the bottom of the box using wood glue and nails, insert the dowels in their holes, then fit the top piece on top of the dowels (see figure 2).

note: You'll find it easier to paint or otherwise finish the inside surfaces and the dowels before you assemble your piece.

# Top Drawer

It's as simple as this: if you're going to the trouble of mounting a shelf, why not get a drawer out of the deal, too? Suddenly, in addition to a ledge for holding large items, you've got brand new drawer space. Fill it with less frequently used items, from holiday tablecloths to birthday candles.

## top drawer step-by-step

THESE INSTRUCTIONS CREATE A TWO-DRAWER UNIT.

### CUT LIST: CASE

| DESCRIPTION | QUANTITY | THICKNESS | WIDTH | LENGTH |
|---|---|---|---|---|
| Sides | 2 | ½" | 3⅛" | 12" |
| Top & Bottom | 2 | ½" | 12" | 25¾" |
| Back | 1 | ¼" plywood | 4⅛" | 25¾" |
| Divider | 1 | ½" | 3⅛" | 12" |

### CUT LIST: DRAWERS

| DESCRIPTION | QUANTITY | THICKNESS | WIDTH | LENGTH |
|---|---|---|---|---|
| Sides | 4 | ½" | 3" | 11⅜" |
| Fronts | 2 | ¾" | 3" | 11" |
| Decorative Front | 2 | ½" | 3" | 12" |
| Ledger Strips | 4 | ⅜" | ½" | 10⅜" |
| Ledger Strips | 4 | ⅜" | ½" | 10" |
| Bottoms | 2 | ¼" plywood | 11" | 10⅜" |
| Backs | 2 | ½" | 3" | 11" |

For metric equivalents, see the chart on page 143.

## MATERIALS & TOOLS

- 8d finish nails
- Washer-head wood screws
- ⅝-inch wire nails, 18 gauge
- Sandpaper
- ½-inch round-head wood screws
- Wood glue
- Wood filler
- Measuring tools
- Circular saw
- Jigsaw
- Hammer
- Nail set

## INSTRUCTIONS: DRAWERS

1. Cut all your pieces to size.

2. Brush a little wood glue on the edges of the pieces, and nail the top and bottom to the sides.

3. Center the divider in the case, and nail it through the top and bottom. Check the case for squareness, then nail the back in place.

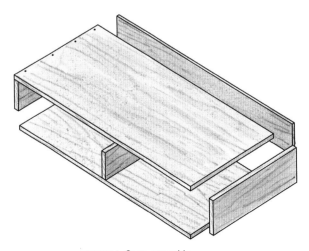

**FIGURE 1.** Case assembly

1. Before cutting your drawer pieces, check the drawer opening measurements on the case. Make any adjustment to the drawer dimensions, if necessary, then cut the material to size. You should allow a ⅛-inch clearance side to side and top to bottom.

2. With the jigsaw, cut U-shaped openings in all the fronts.

3. Using wood glue, assemble the sides to the fronts and backs. Nail the ledgers in place, as shown in figure 2, then glue the bottoms to the ledgers.

4. Position the decorative fronts (which hide the drawer box joints), and screw them in place from the inside.

5. Ease the edges of the case with sandpaper, and slide the drawers into their slots.

6. Finish your drawers and case in any decorative style you like, then mount the unit with purchased metal shelf brackets.

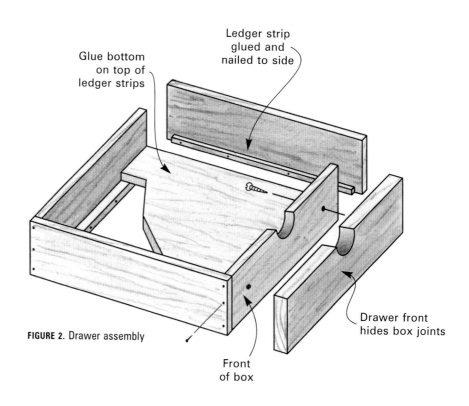

Glue bottom on top of ledger strips

Ledger strip glued and nailed to side

Drawer front hides box joints

**FIGURE 2.** Drawer assembly

Front of box

FOLKS WHO FLIP PANCAKES WITH ONE HAND AND POUR COFFEE WITH THE OTHER don't have time to mess around with inefficient storage systems. Odds are, it was a short-order cook and a waitress working the early-morning shift who originally came up with the idea of vertical dish-ware storage. Shop restaurant supply stores and auctions for a piece like this one, and breakfast at your place will never be the same again.

# salvage solutions

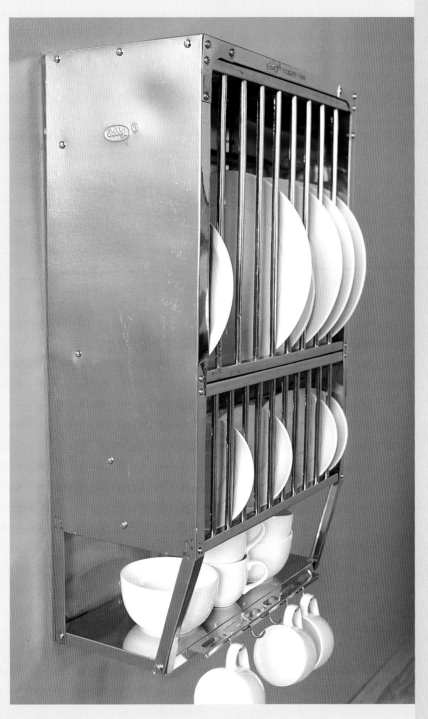

# bedrooms

WE ASK AN AWFUL LOT OF OUR BED-
ROOMS, WHERE STORAGE SPACE IS
OFTEN AT A PREMIUM. Not only do we
require that they hold all we need to keep
us rested, clothed, and adorned, but out
of necessity, many of us also call on our
bedrooms to double as gyms, home
offices, television-viewing spots, and
libraries. Making the most of the storage
options you've got—such as more effectively using the space under the bed or
along a wall—is the first step toward turning your bedroom into the sanctuary it was
meant to be. Next, add clever features,
from closet organizers to mounted nightstands, and you'll clear the way completely for sweet, uncluttered dreams.

# wall-mount nightstand

Logical or not, most of us need a fair number of accessories to help us close our eyes and do nothing: a book or two, a lamp to read by, a glass of water, perhaps some hand lotion, and, alas, an alarm clock to tell us when it's time to get up. And, because we need these props when we're already snug in our beds, we want them not merely nearby, but right at our fingertips. No wonder nightstands are one of a home's most essential short-term storage pieces.

This streamlined wall-mount version converts a hotel towel rack into a handy bedside nesting place for magazines, papers, books, and an easy-to-build wooden tray that serves as a tiny table. Hotel and restaurant suppliers sell the racks. Follow the steps below for adding a tray.

## tray table step-by-step

### MATERIALS & TOOLS

- Cardboard (Break down a box for recycling.)
- Scrap lumber (You can purchase a short length of a 1-inch-thick [2.5 cm] board or a small panel of ½-inch [1.3 cm] or thicker plywood at most home improvement stores if you don't have a selection of scrap lumber to choose from.)
- Lath strip (optional)
- Ruler
- Pencil
- Handsaw
- Hammer
- Finishing nails
- Nail set
- Wood glue
- Wood filler
- Wood finish or paint (optional)

### INSTRUCTIONS

1. Measure the depth and width of the largest shelf on the rack. The tray you create should balance comfortably on the shelf. For it to stay safely in place, it shouldn't be more than half again as deep as the shelf.

2. Use cardboard to create a tray template and try it out on the shelf. Adjust the width and depth as needed.

3. Trace the template on your lumber, and cut out the tray with the handsaw.

4. Measure and cut two lengths of lath strip equal to the depth of your tray.

5. Run a thin line of wood glue on one side of the tray, and nail the lath strip to the side. Repeat for the opposite side.

6. Measure the total width of the tray, including the lath strips. Cut two lengths of lath equal to that length. Glue and nail the strips to the tray.

7. Use the nail set to set the nails. Fill the holes with wood filler and finish the tray any way you like.

# reading pouches

Maybe your smaller bedside necessities aren't the issue. You've got a little table that does a perfect job of storing them close at hand. It's all those saved Sunday papers and back issues of favorite magazines forming an obstacle course on the floor that are the problem. Here's a creative way to tuck them out of sight without giving up the convenience of having them within arm's reach.

## reading pouch step-by-step

### MATERIALS & TOOLS

- 1½ yards (1.35 m) canvas or other heavy fabric (Cut lengthwise, and you can create two two-tiered pouches from this amount.)
- Heavy thread (quilting)
- Standard measuring and marking tools
- Sewing machine
- Heavy needles, size 90/14
- Unless otherwise noted, use a ½-inch (1.3 cm) seam allowance for all seams.

### INSRUCTIONS

1. Cut a rectangle from the canvas measuring 18 x 53 inches (45.7 x 134.6 cm). Finish the raw edges by serging and zigzagging.

2. With the right sides together, seam together the 18-inch (45.7 cm) edges to form a large tube. Press the seam flat.

3. Turn the tube wrong side out and press under a ½-inch (1.3 cm) hem on the serged edges of the tube.

4. From the right side, stitch the hem in place. For added interest, use a decorative thread and/or stitches. Press the hem to set the stitching.

5. Place the tube on a large, flat surface with the 18-inch (45.7 cm) seam to the back. With your marking tool, draw two lines, one 2 inches (5.1 cm) down from the top and the other 14 inches (35.6 cm) down from the top.

6. Stitch on these lines with a multi-motion stitch. Sewing the top line creates the rod pocket, and the bottom line creates the two pouches.

You can hang your pouches from a curtain rod positioned above your headboard or from towel bars installed beside your bed.

# it's
# the
# little
# things

**problem:**

*If I pack it up and put it away, I'll never know which box it's in when I need it.* (It's one of the most common anti-storage arguments ever—and the flawed thinking behind keeping absolutely everything out in the open.)

**solution:**

The answer is amazingly obvious but often overlooked. Tags, stickers, and stamps give any anonymous sea of storage containers—whether plastic ware full of food in the freezer or cardboard boxes of memorabilia in the attic—the labels you need to make sense of them at a quick glance.

# storage straps

Certain clothing items and accessories play by their own rules. If you've ever folded up a silk scarf, put it in a drawer, and told it to stay, you know this. Before long, it's stretched itself out and begun mingling with all the nearby slips and nightgowns. Good news: you can hold hard-to-contain articles like these gently but firmly in place on the inside of a bedroom or closet door. Just use elastic straps much like the ones that do the same job inside suitcases.

## storage straps step-by-step

### MATERIALS & TOOLS

- No-roll elastic, 1¼ inches (3.2 cm) wide (sold with sewing notions)
- Plastic tack glides (Look for these in the hardware store. They're also called furniture glides.)
- Ruler
- Scissors
- Hammer

### INSTRUCTIONS

1. Measure the width of your door. If your door has a central flat panel, measure just the width of the panel. Cut lengths of the no-roll elastic to size.

2. Anchor a length of elastic to the door with a plastic tack glide at each end. Then anchor the center portion of the elastic with two or three evenly spaced glides. Use the hammer to securely fasten the glides to the door.

3. Attach additional lengths of elastic in the same manner. Space them at least 12 inches (30.5 cm) apart.

# canvas shelf covers

Open shelving offers a resourceful alternative for storing all sorts of bedroom items, from extra sheets and blankets to shoes and folded cloths. The only downside is that having everything on full display can make even the neatest room feel cluttered. Fortunately, some basic fabric flaps are all you need to reinstate calm and order.

## shelf cover step-by-step

### MATERIALS & TOOLS

- Canvas, duck cloth, denim, or a similar sturdy fabric (The amount will depend on the size and number of shelves you want to cover.)
- Interfacing (medium-weight fusible or sew-in)
- Fabric for lining (contrasting, if you like)
- Decorative snaps or grommets
- Standard measuring and marking tools
- Sewing machine and needles, size 90
- Thread
- Iron
- Tools for attaching snaps or grommets
- Tacks, nails, or hook-and-loop tape

### INSTRUCTIONS

1. Determine the size of the fabric pieces you need to cut for each cover. First, measure your shelf openings. Next, add a ½-inch (1.3 cm) seam allowance to all sides. Finally, make the pieces approximately 2 inches (5.1 cm) longer (measuring from top to bottom). You'll use the extra fabric to attach the covers to the inside tops of the shelves.

2. Cut out your pieces for the first cover. Lay the main fabric right side up and place the interfacing on top of it. If you're using fusible interfacing, fuse it to the wrong side of the main fabric at this point. Last, place the lining fabric right side down on top of the interfacing to form a fabric "sandwich." NOTE: You can omit the interfacing if your main fabric is stiff or if you want a softer look.

3. Stitch around three sides of the cover using a ½-inch (1.3 cm) seam allowance. Grade the seam allowances, and trim the corners at an angle, then press the seams to set the stitching.

4. Turn the cover right side out, press the seams again, and turn the raw edges inside and stitch the final edge closed. If you like, you can add decorative topstitching to the edges.

5. Attach your snap or grommet, following the directions on the piece's packaging.

6. You can attach the cover to the shelf by tacking or nailing it to the inside of the top of the shelf. You can also use hook-and-loop tape, which makes your covers easy to remove for washing. Stitch the loop side to the top edge of the right side of the cover and tack the hook side to the inside top of the shelf. Repeat steps 2 through 6 for each cover you want to create.

# it's the little things

**problem:**

Too little surface space for storing all of the extras that end up in the bedroom, from pocket change and mail to telephones and remote controls.

**solution:**

Buy a bench or two—or more. Position a small bench on top of a dresser or night table, and you add a level of surface space. Stack a series of benches, and you've got an instant bookshelf. Line up a few low benches on the floor of your closet, and you've got a makeshift shelf for a second layer of shoes. Bonus: benches come in every style imaginable, from paint-cracked country to primary-colored contemporary.

# baskets
# &boxes
# &bins

**THERE'S AN ELEMENT OF KARMA TO**
clothing storage: how you put
pieces away affects what they
look like when you pull them
back out again. Plenty of items,
from cotton T-shirts and cash-
mere sweaters to shawls and
hiking shorts, perform best when
they're folded with care and
neatly stacked away. Cardboard
file boxes, metal foot lockers, plastic containers, and lidded wicker
baskets all make it easy to sort
your clothes by type (and even
color and style), and to label what
you've packed away, if you'd like.

## under-bed storage

Supposedly, human beings began raising their beds up off of cold, drafty floors centuries ago so they'd be warmer when they slept. But any child who has ever heard the words, *You're not going out to play until this room is picked up*, knows the *real* value of a bed with some wide open space underneath it. In that concealed area where many of us once shoved stuffed animals and plastic game pieces as fast as our little hands could sweep across the floor, we can now slide metal boxes, rattan baskets, and rolling platforms made to store our more grown-up possessions.

Check specialty stores and mail-order catalogs for trays and chests designed especially for under-bed storage. You can typically find variations in cardboard, plastic, and wood, with features such as dividers and see-through, zippered vinyl covers. To fashion your own simple under-bed rolling drawer, nail 1 x 4 strips to the edges of a ⅝-inch (1.6 cm) plywood bottom, add wood blocks and casters to the corners, and attach a drawer pull to each side.

# hanging hooks

IMAGINE HOW MUCH BETTER YOU'D BE AT STORING things in their proper places if doing so didn't involve opening doors and searching for hangers or—worse—folding a sweater or shirt you're just going to wear again sometime soon. Bedrooms are full of opportunities for bypassing all those fussy, time-consuming storage approaches and simply suspending things from that friendliest of storage devices, the hook. We created the mirror shown here, adorned with knobs and handles successfully posing as hooks, as a holding place for hats, scarves, and other small items. You could easily adjust the size of both the mirror and the hooks to make a version better suited for hanging clothes.

**HAPPY TO HANG FROM HOOKS**

- Bathrobes
- Workout clothes
- Caps
- Sunglasses on a string
- The sweats you put on every night after work
- Neckties
- Bathing suits
- Pajamas
- Belts
- Purses and bags
- Necklaces & bracelets

## hooked mirror step-by-step

**MATERIALS & TOOLS**

- Wooden picture frame
- Drawer pulls and knobs
- Mirror, cut to fit
- Wood stain or paint (optional)
- Screwdriver (optional)
- Pliers (optional)
- Pencil
- Electric drill and bits

**INSTRUCTIONS**

1. Choose an inexpensive wooden picture frame with a profile that pleases you. A frame with a broad, flat face works best, but there's no reason a more complex frame face wouldn't work as well with a bit more planning.

2. Remove the glass and any push points in the frame. If you're planning to stain or paint the frame, do it now before you drill holes and install the hardware you've chosen.

3. Plan the placement of your knobs and handles on the bottom of the frame.

4. Mark the placement on the back side of the frame. This ensures that your screw placement doesn't interfere with the inner lip of the frame.

5. Choose a drill bit equal to or slightly larger than the screws included with your knobs and handles. Drill the number of holes you need.

6. Attach your knobs and handles, along with whatever hanging hardware came with your frame, insert the mirror, and mount your new organizer.

# quilt rack storage

Sturdy wooden racks like these—designed as display stands for quilts and blankets—come in a range of sizes and styles. But because of their handsome look, they're also willing and able accomplices when you need to disguise a storage solution as bedroom decoration. If you're short on closet space, they offer an appealing way to store linens, towels, extra blankets, and even overflow clothes right out in the open.

OKAY, YOU'VE RESIGNED YOURSELF TO THE FACT THAT YOU'RE NEVER going to change. Clothes will be tossed, not hung. Shoes will be mounded, not lined up. Books will be piled, not shelved. You accept yourself and you're at peace with your casual approach to storage. But you'd also like to one day be able to see your bedroom floor again. Here's an easy compromise even you can live with. Make a few galvanized tubs the targets for all of your tossing, mounding, and piling. They'll contribute a relaxed sense of order without cramping your carefree style.

KIDS THINK OF THEIR ROOMS AS THE
CENTER OF THEIR UNIVERSE—their very
own place where they can invite friends, invent
games, hide out, play, learn, and express exactly who they are. The only problem is, all of that
expression can create an awful lot of chaos. If
you want to encourage both spirited individual-
ity and order at the same time, you need storage solutions that are easy to reach, interesting
to use, bright, fun—and as welcoming and inviting as the toys and games they contain.

# kids' rooms

# string 'em up

Spend enough time standing ankle deep in a sea of scattered game pieces, cast-off socks, and stuffed animals that seem to multiply overnight, and it will eventually dawn on you that that big blank wall is much more than a vital support structure. It's your answer to getting some of the mess off the floor and out of the way. String a wire from point A to point B, and you've got a clever indoor clothesline that becomes an accessible place to hang the coats and jackets you reach for at least once a day. Add some colorful plastic clips, and you can also use the wire to suspend everything from cards and drawings to a collection of teddy bears.

### string 'em up step-by-step

1. Screw two small metal cleats (the same kind you might see keeping ropes and cords in place on a boat) into the wall. Space them about 8 or 10 feet (2.5 or 3 m) apart and set them at a height you can comfortably reach.

2. Select a cord you like (home improvement stores carry all sorts of varieties), hitch it to the cleats, and your hanging storage system is ready to go.

BONUS: If you tire of the look, you can remove the cord and use the cleats as coat hooks.

# stacked storage unit

Treat these basic wooden boxes like big, hollow building blocks, and you can stack your way toward order. Use the boxes on the bottom to store books, balls, action figures, and other small toys and accessories you want your little ones to be able to get to all by themselves. Reserve those on top for messy art supplies and toys that require some supervision. You can stack your boxes right on top of each other or follow the instructions below for adding sections of wood that separate each level. Just be sure not to pile your boxes too high (typically no more than three in a stack); you don't want to invite your child's inner climber out to play.

## stacked storage unit step-by-step

### CUT LIST

| DESCRIPTION | QUANTITY | THICKNESS | WIDTH | LENGTH |
|---|---|---|---|---|
| Sides | 6 | ¾" | 18" | 16½" |
| Top & Bottom | 6 | ¾" | 18" | 24" |
| Door | 6 | ¾" | 18" | 11¹⁵⁄₁₆" |
| Back | 3 | ¼" plywood | 18" | 24" |
| Dividers | 3 | ¾" | 18" | 16½" |
| Separator (sides) | 1 | 2¾" | 3" | 12" |
| Separator (ends) | 12 | ¾" | 1½" | 3" |
| Locators | 10 | ¾" | 1½" | 10½" |

For metric equivalents, see the chart on page 143.

### MATERIALS & TOOLS

- 8d finish nails
- ⅝-inch wire nails, 18 gauge
- Sandpaper
- Wood glue
- Wood filler
- 12 full overlay hinges (see page 54)
- 12 magnetic catches
- Measuring tools
- Circular saw
- Hammer
- Nail set

### INSTRUCTIONS

1. The process for building these boxes is identical to the one for building the divided case for the Top Drawer project, page 81. Only the dimensions differ. Cut your pieces to size and assemble the open boxes, following the instructions on page 81. You'll add the doors in step 6.

2. Separators (rectangular boxes that are open on their tops and bottoms) provide spacing between the storage boxes. To make them, cut the pieces to size and nail them together, using figure 1 as a guide.

3. Size the locator strips so they fit loosely inside the separators. A clearance of ¹⁄₁₆ inch per side is about right.

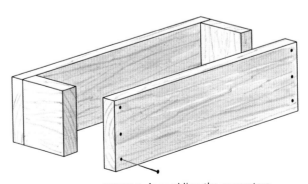

**FIGURE 1.** Assembling the separators

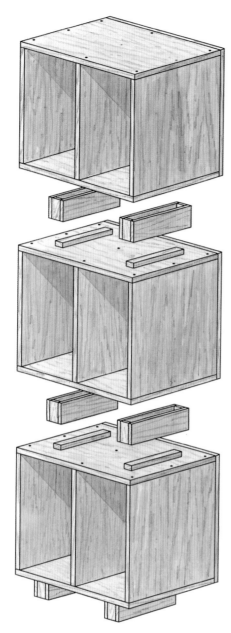

**FIGURE 2.** Stacked Storage Unit assembly

4. Use wire nails to fasten locators to the top and bottom of the bottom and middle boxes and to the bottom of the top box, measuring their placement carefully, so the other pieces will line up evenly and nest together (see figure 2).

5. Test assemble the unit to make sure all the pieces line up (again, figure 2 provides a guide). You don't have to nail any of the separators in place, though you may want to nail the ones you're using under the bottom box to the locators, so the bottom piece is easy to move.

6. Lay the boxes on their backs to mount the doors. Fasten the hinges to the sides of the boxes, 3 inches from the top and bottom on each. Test fit the doors with the hinges before mounting them. Depending on the brand of hinge you use, you may need to adjust the width of the doors slightly. You want a middle gap of about ⅛ inch between doors. Finally, install the magnetic catches, following the manufacturer's instructions.

7. Set any nails that show slightly below the surface. Fill the resulting holes with wood filler. Give the entire assembly a final sanding, and you're ready for finishing. Add surface decoration in any way you choose. Paints, stencils, stamps, a different color on each door, and even chalkboard paint are all options.

LEAVE OLD-FASHIONED WOODEN TOY TRUNKS TO PEOPLE WHO EMPLOY governesses. Tossing everything into one seems like a good idea— until it's time to fish through layers of plastic trucks and baby dolls to get to the missing Lego block at the bottom. Smaller containers are the more manageable way to go. Fill shallow baskets and plastic bins with board games, and slide them under beds. Load larger ones with everything from beach towels to baseball bats, and tuck them into shelf compartments, as we have here. You can also pull in props from other areas of the house. Tool and tackle boxes and even garden totes make excellent containers for Crayons and coloring books or a doll's wardrobe and accessories.

baskets
&
boxes
&
bins

# in the bag

The best thing about these bags is that you can put nearly anything in them, from shoes and sports equipment to dirty laundry (one color-coded bag per kid). The second best thing is that they fold up easily and fit in a suitcase, making them good travel-along pieces for temporary storage at grandma's house or wherever you're going.

## drawstring bag step-by-step

### MATERIALS & TOOLS

- ⅓ yard (.3 m) top fabric
- ¼ yard (.45 m) bottom fabric
- ¼ yard (.22 m) medium interfacing to reinforce the bottom (optional)
- 2 yards (1.8 m) accent ribbon
- 1 yard (.9 m) cord for drawstring
- Standard measuring and marking tool
- Thread
- Sewing machine and needles

### CUTTING

CUT THE FOLLOWING PIECES:

- 1 top piece, 10 x 33 inches (25.4 x 83.8 cm)
- 1 bottom piece, 10 x 33 inches (25.4 x 83.82 cm)
- 1 base piece, 8 x 8 inches (20.3 x 20.3 cm) (If you're using interfacing, cut a second base piece out of fabric and one out of interfacing.)
- 1 loop strip, 2½ x 6 inches (6.4 x 15.2 cm)

Unless otherwise noted, use a ½-inch (1.3 cm) seam allowance for all seams.

## BODY

1. Place the right sides of the top and bottom pieces together. Seam along one 33-inch (83.8 cm) side. Finish the raw edge any way you like, then press the seam to one side.

2. Place the accent ribbon on the right side, centered over the seam you sewed in step 1. Stitch each side of the ribbon down, using decorative thread or stitches, if you like.

3. Fold the body into quarters lengthwise to find four equidistant points along the bottom edge of the bottom piece (for matching up against the square base later). Mark a straight line from each of these points on the bottom edge to a corresponding point on the top edge. Stitch on either side of each line. You should end up with six parallel lines of stitching, each 19 inches (48.3 cm) long (see figure 1).

## LOOP

1. Fold the loop strip in half lengthwise, and press it.

2. Open the strip, place the raw edges on the centerline, and press them.

3. Fold the strip in half again, keeping the raw edges on the centerline, and stitch along each long edge.

## CASING FOR CORD

1. Finish the raw edge at the top of the bag any way you choose.

2. On the inside of that edge, measure in 4 inches (10.2 cm) from one of the parallel lines you marked on the body to find the center point of one side of the bag. Mark it.

3. Fold the loop (from above) in half, position the two ends against the center point you marked in step 2, and sew them in place.

4. Fold the edge of the top of the bag down 1¼ inches (3.2 cm), turn in the finished edge, and stitch along the edge 1 inch (2.5 cm) from the fold. For added strength, stitch again, close to the outside edge.

## ASSEMBLY

1. Fold the body in half, right sides together. Sew along the 19-inch (48.3 cm) side from the bottom to the top. As you reach the casing, taper off the edge of the fabric (see figure 2). This will leave two openings for the bag's cord.

2. Finish the seam and press it to one side.

3. If you're using interfacing, sandwich the interfacing between the two pieces of base fabric. Stitch or fuse it in place.

4. To attach the body of the bag to the base, place the right sides together, matching the corners. Carefully clip into the seam allowance of the body at each corner to square the corners. Stitch the pieces together, using a multistitch on your machine.

5. Finish the raw edges, press the seam, and thread your cord through the casing.

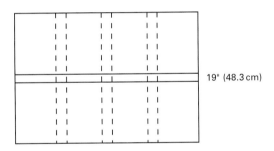

**FIGURE 1.** Create parallel lines of stitching, each 19 inches (48.3 cm).

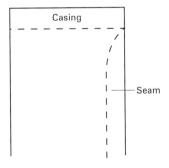

**FIGURE 2.** Taper your stitches off the edge as you reach the casing.

# covered boxes

When coming up with storage solutions for kids' rooms, it's important not to lose sight of the obvious: kids grow and change. As they do, the paraphernalia that fills their rooms changes (train sets and sidewalk chalk give way to computer games and diaries). And so does their taste (blue bunnies are out, turquoise flowers are in). That means you want storage containers that are either inexpensive or adaptable—or both. Ordinary cardboard boxes are about as affordable as you can get—and they come in all kinds of sizes and shapes. Cover them with wallpaper, shelf paper, decorative handmade paper, or even gift wrap, and you can easily tailor them to the mood of the moment.

# covered box step-by-step

## MATERIALS & TOOLS

- Corrugated cardboard box with lid
- Wallpaper (Look in cutout bins for rolls of discontinued wallpaper.)
- Spray adhesive
- Glue stick
- Ribbons and buttons
- Newspaper to cover your work area
- Scissors
- Sharp craft knife
- Ruler
- Pencil
- Hot glue gun and glue sticks

## COVERING THE BOX

1. Unroll the wallpaper, pattern-side down, on a flat surface. Lay the box on its side, and wrap the paper around the box to cover all four sides with an additional 1½ inches (3.8 cm) overlap. Neatly trim the paper to this length.

2. Measure the height of the box. Add 6 inches (15.2 cm) to this measurement for overlap at the top and bottom of the box. Measure and trim the length of wallpaper to this height. If you're covering a small box, you can add a little less than 6 inches (15.2 cm).

3. Cover your work area to protect it. Spray adhesive on one long side of the box, and lay the paper along it, allowing the overlap to fold over a short side of the box.

4. Work around the box, spraying adhesive on each side and pressing the paper flat. When you reach the side with the overlap, lift the overlap, spray the side, and press the overlap down. Use the glue stick to attach the end of the paper to the overlap.

5. Lay the box on its side and use the craft knife to make a straight cut in the paper that extends beyond the box at each corner, up to the base of the box. Fold the flaps over to the base. Miter the corners by drawing a straight line diagonally from corner to corner, across the folded flaps. Trim the paper along these lines with the craft knife. Use the glue stick to adhere the flaps flat.

6. Measure and cut a rectangle of paper that's ½ inch (1.3 cm) smaller than the dimensions of the box base. Spray the rectangle of paper with adhesive, and smooth it into place on the bottom of the box.

7. Lay the box on its side and at each corner, cut into the paper that extends beyond the box, straight down to the edge of the top of the box. Use the glue stick to adhere these flaps to the inside of the box. If your paper is thick, you can trim the paper at a slight angle at each end, so the flaps fit neatly into the corners.

## COVERING THE LID

1. Roll out a length of wallpaper. Lay the lid upside down on the wrong side of the paper, and draw around the outline of the lid. Remove the lid. Use your ruler to straighten the lines if necessary.

2. Measure the depth of the lid. Extend the straight lines of the box lid to equal double the depth of the box. Create ⅜-inch (9.5 mm) side overlaps at each end of the longest sides to wrap around the box. Cut out the entire piece.

3. Spray the lid top with adhesive and carefully center it on the space you traced for the box lid. Use a glue stick to spread glue on the long sides and the overlaps. Press them into place on the outside and inside of the lid. Adhere the shorter sides in the same way.

## ADDING DECORATIVE HANDLES

(These can also serve as helpful color-coded labels for what's inside.)

1. Fold an 8-inch (20 cm) length of grosgrain ribbon in half. Trim the cut ends at a 45° angle.

2. Hot glue the folded ribbon to the box lid. You will need to hot glue between the ribbons as well. Then, hot glue a colorful button to the folded ribbon.

# wall pockets

Hanging pocket organizers like this one are available in both fabric and see-through plastic styles at major chain stores and through toy and children's-furniture catalogs. If you're a sewer, you can also whip up a personalized version to meet your needs perfectly.

## wall pockets step-by-step

### MATERIALS & TOOLS

- 1⅝ yards (1.46 m) canvas or other heavy material
- Heavy thread (quilting)
- Standard measuring and marking tools
- Sewing machine

### BODY

1. Cut a rectangle of fabric 37 x 30 inches (93.98 x 76.2 cm).

2. Turn the edges of all four sides under ½ inch (1.3 cm) twice. This will produce a double hem. Press it and sew it in place.

3. Fold the top edge over 2 inches (5.1 cm), and press it. Sew the folded edge on the wrong side to create the top hem.

### TABS

1. Cut two strips, each 3 x 6 inches (7.6 x 15.2 cm). Fold each in half and press the wrong sides together.

2. Open the strips, place the raw edges on the centerline, and press them.

3. Fold the strips in half again, keeping the raw edges on the centerline, and stitch along each long edge. Place the tabs on the wrong side of the body, about 1 inch (2.5 cm) in from each edge, with the loops extended above the top edge. Sew them in place.

### POCKETS

1. Cut three rectangles, each 10 x 57 inches (25.4 x 144.8 cm).

2. Turn all four sides of each under ½ inch (1.3 cm) twice, to again produce a double hem. Each should now measure approximately 8 x 55 inches (20.3 x 139.7 cm).

3. Determine the bottom edge. (If the fabric has a nap, orient the pockets with the nap going up.)

4. Baste pleats in place along the bottom edge (see figure 1 for placement). Press them.

### ASSEMBLY

1. Place the top edge of the first rectangle 4 inches (10.2 cm) down from the top of the body. Sew along the sides and bottom, using a multi-motion stitch. Sew slowly over the pleats, which include several layers of fabric. Finally, sew down the center of each pleat to form three separate pockets.

2. Place the top edge of the second rectangle ½ inch (1.3 cm) below the bottom of the first row. Sew it in place and stitch the pocket divisions, as described in step 1.

3. Place the top edge of the third rectangle ½ inch (1.3 cm) below the bottom of the second row, and sew it as described in step 1.

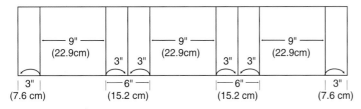

Figure 1. Pleat placement

# bathrooms

WHEN YOU'RE IN THE BATHROOM, CHANCES
ARE YOU'VE GOT SOAP ON YOUR HANDS,
toothpaste in your mouth, or a towel wrapped
around your dripping body. That means this is
not the place where you want to do a lot of
strategic maneuvering to find or get to what you
need, whether it's your contact solution or your
kids' bath toys. At the same time, you typically
don't want everything spread out in full view in
this tiniest room in the house. Strategic sorting
and clever grouping are the keys to successful
bathroom storage. Contain those groupings in
some of the following ways, and you'll arrive at
the blissful conclusion that accessibility and tran-
quility can co-exist.

## storing with style

No one ever said storage solutions had to be extravagant to look absolutely elegant. This bathroom makes beautiful use of some of the simplest and least expensive storage ideas ever. The wooden peg rail, with enough knobs for towels, robes, hanging soaps, and a mirror, is much more useful than a single towel rack. A sliding caddy in the tub holds all the accessories a bather needs, while wooden bowls of various sizes perform a similar function at the sink. Tiny flea market tables provide space for overflow items and a few decorative touches.

# hooks & ladder

A propped ladder outfitted with hooks and hanging bags can go a long way toward stepping-up your bathroom's storage potential. Each rung takes on part of the load that overstuffed closets and cabinets can no longer bear. Go with a contemporary metal ladder like this one (which we've anchored in place by standing the legs in the holes of cored bricks). Or, for a rustic look, use a plain wooden ladder.

**problem:**

Storage solutions that seem to add to the clutter they're supposed to be containing

**solution:**

Unify, unify, unify. Keeping in mind that order is frequently in the eye of the beholder, cut down on drastic variations in color, pattern, and style of storage containers. If you've got everything in its place, but one of those places is a purple bin, the other is a checkered hamper, and the third is a series of yellow-and-green baskets, the look—in your one small bathroom space—probably won't be harmonious. Try using storage containers that are all the same size, shape, or shade, and stay away from pieces with competing patterns.

it's
the
little
things

# shelving

In an ideal world, you'd have a walk-in linen closet just off the bathroom, where you'd store perfectly folded stacks of towels and all sorts of other supplies, from toilet paper and extra soap to candles and bath oil. But back in your reality-based house, every inch of closet space is in heavy demand, and the most your bathroom offers is a small cabinet or two. What to do about the towels, toilet paper, and the rest? Set yourself up with some bathroom shelves.

The same shelving units we typically associate with kitchens or living rooms can easily expand your bathroom's storage capacity. At home stores, you can find tall, narrow, free-standing structures, small wall-mount designs, and nearly everything in between. Many models come equipped with added features such as towel racks, bin inserts, or rolling wheels. It's also easy to customize plain units with those sorts of additions yourself. Or, you can build exactly what you want from scratch by adapting one of the shelf projects from Chapter 2, beginning on page 20.

THESE HANDY SLOTTED CONTAINERS LOOK AS IF THEY ONCE
helped sort the mail in an office or organize a department
store display. Whatever their origin, their divided compartments are just the thing for keeping all the lotions, pow-
ders, oils, and tonics that belong in a bathroom in order. If
you like the look but can't find used units like these, adapt
the Bin Shelf design, page 29, to make your own. It's a simple matter of lengthening the shelf, straightening
the brackets, and adding dividers where you want them.

salvage
solutions

## clearing countertops

Three things are true about much bathroom storage. First, it's short term. You're not stowing the comb and hand mirror away until next year; you just need a place to put them until later in the day. Second, it often involves small objects, such as hair clips and pill bottles. And third, because those objects are so small and because you're going to use them all again soon, it seems most convenient to keep them right there on the countertop. This, of course, is the problem. Soon, every inch of counter space is covered and you can't find a thing.

Fortunately, the solution is as simple as scooping up similar items and storing them together in countertop containers. Here's an imaginative one for holding tooth-brushes, makeup brushes, or anything with a long, narrow handle. To make your own, stack a common cored brick (you know, the kind with holes in it) atop a paver brick (the kind without holes). Use contrasting colors of brick, buy bricks in the same shade, or paint your bricks to match your bathroom.

## hanging hamper step-by-step

### MATERIALS & TOOLS

- Canvas or heavy cotton laundry bag
- Grommet kit (Heavy-duty ¾-inch [1.9 cm] grommets work well. Look for grommet kits in the fastener aisle of home improvement stores. You may also be able to find them in the notions area of well-stocked fabric stores.)
- Heavy-duty cup hooks (two per bag)
- 1-inch (2.5 cm) or larger split rings (two per bag)
- Snap links
- Wooden cutting board
- Hammer
- Craft knife
- Electric drill and bits

### INSTRUCTIONS

1. Lay your bag on a flat surface. Spread it out flat. Determine the placement of the grommets. If your bag has a drawstring, be sure to place your grommets below the case for the cord.

2. Follow the manufacturer's instructions for setting the grommets. This requires some force, so work on a wooden cutting board so you don't mar the surface of your table. You'll probably need a hammer to strike the metal rod used to set the grommets and a craft knife to trim the fabric from the center of the set grommets.

3. Hold your bag up against the wall where you intend to hang it. Use a pencil to lightly mark the location of the grommets. Drill pilot holes for the cup hooks where you made the marks. If necessary, use plastic wall anchors to secure the hooks in the wall.

4. Slip a split ring on each hook, then use snap links to connect the bag to the rings.

## hanging hampers

If your bathroom is smaller than you'd like, it follows that you've probably got less floor space than you need. Certain things aren't moving: your toilet and tub to name just two. But others offer you a bit more flexibility. Dangle laundry hampers from hooks on the wall, for example, and you free up precious square footage for the wastebasket and the bathroom scale.

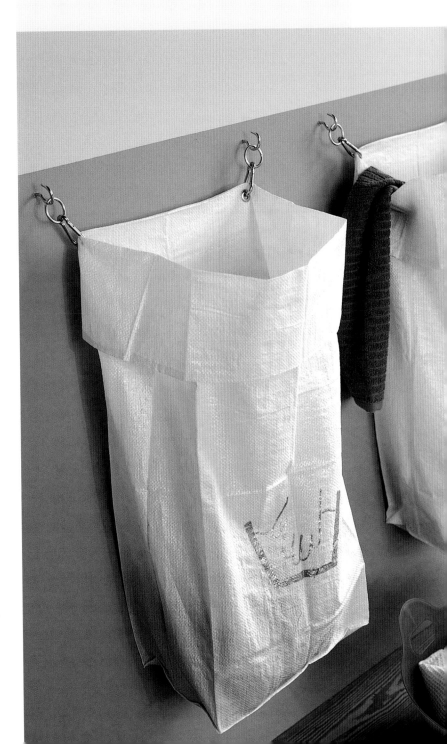

# towel latch

A good storage system for in-use towels is one that's hung at a reachable height near the water source. That's all that's technically required, but it's always nice when it can have some distinctive style, too. This one gets its modern—and appropriately aquatic—flair from the PVC tubing used to create water hoses.

## towel latch step-by-step

THESE INSTRUCTIONS CREATE A UNIT WITH THREE TOWEL LATCHES.

### MATERIALS & TOOLS

- 1½ yards (1.4 m) of ½-inch (1.3 cm) high-pressure braided PVC tubing (You'll find this in the plumbing section and can choose from clear, white, or black.)
- 24-inch (61 cm) length of 1 x 12-inch pine board
- 3-foot (.9 m) length of ¾ x 2-inch pine board
- Scrap wood block
- 3 ⅝-inch (1.6 cm) washers
- 4 screws for mounting (See page 23 for choosing the appropriate screw type for your wall.)
- Finishing nails
- Wood filler
- Acrylic paint
- Paintbrush
- Cyanoacrylate glue; use a glue suitable for use with metal
- Sandpaper
- Scissors
- Ruler
- Handsaw
- Electric drill and bits
- ¾-inch (1.9 cm) spade bit
- Staple gun and staples
- Hammer
- Nail set
- Pencil

### INSTRUCTIONS

1. Measure and cut three 18-inch (45.7 cm) lengths of the braided PVC tubing. Set them aside.

2. Measure and mark the horizontal centerline of the 1 x 12 pine board. Measure and mark three points at 6-inch (15.2 cm) intervals along the centerline.

3. Use the drill and spade bit to bore the three holes you marked in step 2, placing a scrap wood block behind the board to prevent splintering or accidently boring a hole into your work surface.

4. Sand any rough edges, and paint the board as desired.

5. Center and glue the washers over the holes. Let them dry.

6. Fold a length of PVC tubing in half and pull the ends through one of the holes. Flatten the ends of the tubing and staple them securely on the back side of the board, one end on each side of the hole. Repeat with the remaining lengths of tubing.

7. Use the handsaw to cut the ¾ x 2-inch wood strip into two equal lengths, each 18 inches (45.7 cm) long. These are your wall cleats.

8. Mount the wall cleats on the wall using the appropriate mounting hardware. Space them 5 inches (12.7 cm) apart.

9. Center the 1 x 12 board on the cleats and use finishing nails to attach it. Use the nail set to set the nails. Fill the holes with wood putty and touch up the paint.

# garden sheds, garages & workshops

**MAYBE YOU'VE GOT AN ACTUAL SHED OR WORKSHOP.**
Or perhaps your version is a corner of an unfinished basement
where you pot the occasional plant, or a spot in the garage
where you keep your hammer and picture-hanging nails. Either
way, most of us need a designated area for rigging, repairing, and
general puttering—and for keeping all the miscellany involved.
Since these areas are meant to support our need for therapeu-
tic tinkering, we don't want clearing a path to what's in them
to be a frustrating project all its own. To the rescue: easy ideas
for keeping these catchall stations organized and functional.

# keeping track of tools & supplies

Like cooking utensils and art supplies, tools are a whole lot more fun to use if you don't have to scrounge around in a big, cavernous container to find the one you need. Taking a cue from the sectioned pockets of a good tool belt, these hanging bags help you divide what you've got into logical groups, then store each bunch separately and in clear view.

## tool bag step-by-step

### MATERIALS & TOOLS

- "Stuff" sacks (These water-resistant sacks are available in a variety of sizes wherever you find outdoor trekking equipment. From 4 to 18 inches tall [10.2 to 45.7 cm], they come in an eye-popping variety of bright colors.)
- 1 plastic spring clamp per sack
- Heavy corrugated board (optional)
- Plastic washers
- Screws (drywall or masonry, depending on the type of wall you have)
- Electric drill and bits
- Craft knife (optional)
- Screwdriver or screw bit for an electric drill
- Level

### INSTRUCTIONS

1. Select a drill bit that matches the size screws you purchased, and drill a hole in one arm of each spring clamp.

2. If you want to create a firm bottom for each sack, trace and cut out a circle on cardboard, slightly smaller than the bottom of each sack. If you're going to store something particularly heavy, go ahead and cut a second circle to give the sack's bottom additional strength.

3. Mark a level line on the wall. Attach each clamp to the wall with a plastic washer and screw, creating a row of evenly spaced spring clamps. Add as many rows as you need, then clamp the bags in place.

IT'S HUMAN NATURE. WE'RE ALL A lot more likely to put something away if getting it to its place—and back out again—isn't a major endeavor. Rather than lug bags of mulch here and pet food there, give each of your bulky, heavy supplies its own container, equip it with casters, and wheel what you need where you want it to go. Simply follow the instructions for adding casters to indoor furniture (page 41) to make trash cans, plastic pots, tin tubs, and even small work-surface containers mobile.

# garden storage

You can argue that the best gardens are not the ones in which everything is confined to neat, organized rows. But even if sprawling vines and random patches of blooms are what you're after in the end, you'll have more fun getting there if you've got some order behind the scenes. With a couple of easy additions, this basic wooden shelving unit—the kind you might buy for holding books in the bedroom—becomes a storage case for gardening supplies and a handy potting table all in one.

Create a bin on the bottom for bags of bulbs and other bulky items by simply nailing a purchased piece of fencing or lattice over half of the lowest shelf opening. To make a place for seed packets or garden plans to hang temporarily, pound tiny nails into the front edge of one of the higher shelves, and use paper clips to attach the packets or papers. You can even add cup hooks to the side of your shelving unit if you also want a place for hanging your gardening gloves and hat. Finally, follow the steps here to install a fold-out ledge for potting plants.

## potting ledge step-by-step

### CUT LIST

| DESCRIPTION | QTY. | THICKNESS | WIDTH | LENGTH |
|---|---|---|---|---|
| Ledge | 3 | ¾" | 4" | ⅛" shorter than length of shelf opening |
| Ledge Cleat | 2 | ¾" | 4" | 12" |
| Shelf Support | 2 | ¾" | 2" | Same as shelf depth |

For metric equivalents, see the chart on page 143.

### MATERIALS & TOOLS

- Wooden bookcase
- 1¼-inch wire nails, 18 gauge
- 8d finish nails
- Sandpaper
- 2 barrel bolts
- 2 ¾-inch inset hinges or 2 butt hinges, 3 inches wide x 1¾ inches
- Chain (for door support)
- Measuring tools
- Table saw
- Wood glue
- Wood filler
- Hammer

### INSTRUCTIONS

1. Lay the three ledge boards edge to edge, making certain the ends are all flush. Using wood glue and wire nails, fasten them together with the ledge cleats. (See figure 1.)

2. Determine which shelf you want the ledge to attach to. Underneath that shelf, glue and nail the shelf supports in place, with their tops flush against the bottom of the shelf and their front edges flush to the front edge of the bookcase. Nail through the shelf into the supports, as well.

3. Following the manufacturers instructions, install the inset or butt hinges on the cleats of the ledge and on the supported shelf. The ledge should close so that the face of the cleats and the front edge of the bookcase are flush.

4. Install a barrel bolt on each cleat, approximately 1½ inches from the top edge of the cleat.

5. Install a chain running from the inside of one side of the bookcase to the top inside corner of the same side of the ledge. The length of the chain you need will depend on how it's mounted. It should be attached to the bookcase side approximately 2 inches in from the front edge and 12 inches up from the shelf that's attached to the ledge. If you want your ledge to support heavier loads, attach a chain on each side.

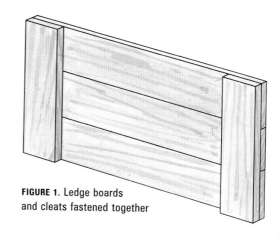

**FIGURE 1.** Ledge boards and cleats fastened together

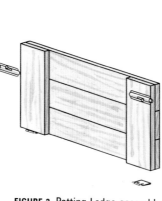

**FIGURE 2.** Potting Ledge assembly

**problem:**

Paint chips, plant-care cards, the receipt for the curtain rod that's the wrong size. Where in the workshop or shed—where clean, clear surface space is scant—can you store these important slips of paper?

**solution:**

Purchase a narrow strip of wooden trellis, prop it or hang it somewhere at eye level, and use clothespins to clip your scraps in place where you can't miss them.

it's
the
little
things

## chainlink organizer

It's spatial relations 101. Whether you're being crowded out by camping lanterns and backpacks or watering cans and dog leashes, chances are you've got a bunch of stuff that would take up a lot less space if you could just find a way to store it all in one tall tower rather than lined up, side-by-side, on a shelf. Easy enough. Suspend a strong chain with large links from a sturdy hook up high, add a collection of clips, and you've got a vertical organizer that helps you rearrange all sorts of matter.

# key corral

Think of all the things that need to be locked up: the house, the cars, the bikes, the storage shed, the family locker at the gym, and the neighbor's house after you feed the cat and water the plants. Multiply those things by the number of people who do all the locking and unlocking, from the teenager who now drives, to the house guests who need to be able to let themselves in and out. Suddenly, you begin to understand how that scrambled set of unmarked keys you keep in an overcrowded drawer came to be. A personalized key corral offers a much more systematic way to store them all. Hang it just inside the garage, and it's easy for people to pick up and drop off keys as they come and go.

## key corral step-by-step

### MATERIALS & TOOLS

- Piece of plywood big enough to hold all your hooks (Most home improvement centers have precut sections of plywood, so you don't have to purchase—and carry—an unwieldy full sheet.)
- Wood stain or diluted acrylic paint (optional)
- Sawtooth mirror hanger
- Bulldog clips
- ⅜-inch (9.5 mm) wood screws
- Flat washers (the size will depend on the size of your bulldog clips)
- Cup hooks
- Handsaw
- Ruler
- Pencil
- Screwdriver

### INSTRUCTIONS

1. If necessary, measure, mark, and trim your plywood to size.

2. Stain the plywood if you like, and let it dry.

3. Center and attach the mirror hanger 3 inches (7.6 cm) from the top of the board on the back.

4. Make as many rows as you need of marks for bulldog clips and for cup hooks. Space the marks at regular intervals, and position each new row approximately 4½ inches (11.4 cm) below the one above it.

5. Use flat washers and wood screws to attach bulldog clips to the first row of marks and to every other row after it.

6. Screw cup hooks into the marks on the rows below the clips.

7. Use the clips to label each hook. Here, we've used photos of the people whose keys will hang from each hook and, for common keys, of the items the keys go with. You could also cut out pieces of card stock and decorate them with stamped or stenciled symbols (one for car, another for house), or let each key holder paint or hand letter his or her name.

# patterns

### basic shelf bracket patterns

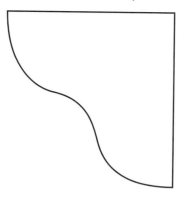

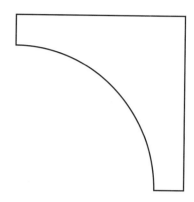

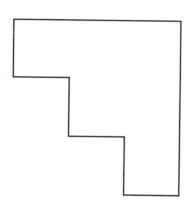

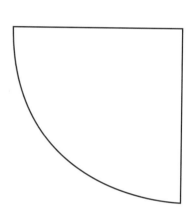

### basic ledge bracket pattern

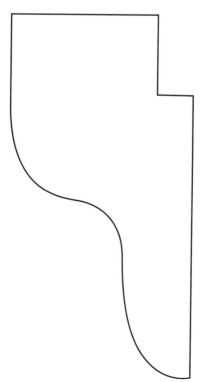

satchel side pattern

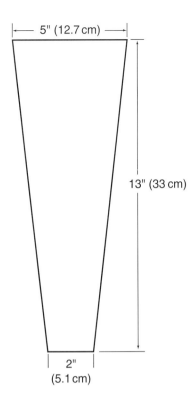

5" (12.7 cm)

13" (33 cm)

2"
(5.1 cm)

bin self bracket pattern

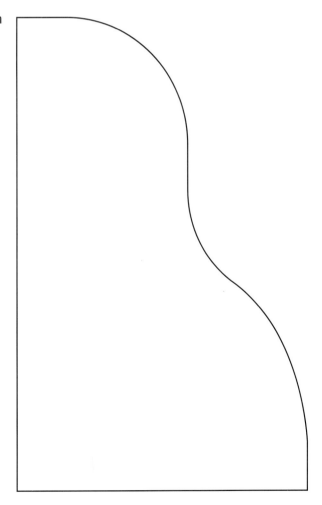

# contributors

This outstanding team helped develop the sewing, woodworking, and general do-it-yourself projects that appear throughout the book.

**KAREN M. BENNETT** has been a member of the Southern Highland Craft Guild since 1983. She teaches tatting, sewing, and needle arts, and also sells her pieces to galleries. Recently, she has become a Bernina instructor for the company's local dealership. Karen's work has been featured in numerous Lark books.

Now retired to his dream shop in the mountains of western North Carolina, **MIKE CALLIHAN** is a graduate mechanical engineer who earned his living in the plastic injection molding industry. His first love in woodworking is building all manner of furniture, ranging in style from Shaker to classic 18th-century reproductions. Though he has no formal training in furniture building, Mike grew up in the woodworking industry, working in his father's cabinet shop. In addition to furniture building, he enjoys woodcarving, turning, and cabinetmaking.

**TERRY TAYLOR** lives and works in Asheville, North Carolina, as an editor and project coordinator for Lark Books. He is a prolific designer and exhibiting artist and works in media ranging from metals and jewelry to paper crafts and mosaics.

# acknowledgments

Thanks to **CHRIS BRYANT** and **SKIP WADE** and **TERRY TAYLOR** and **JEFF WEBB**, who opened their beautifully organized homes to our cameras.

Images on pages 17, 18, and 62 appear courtesy of **HOLD EVERYTHING**.

| INCHES | CENTIMETERS | | INCHES | CENTIMETERS |
|---|---|---|---|---|
| ⅛ | 3 mm | | 12 | 30 |
| ¼ | 6 mm | | 13 | 32.5 |
| ⅜ | 9 mm | | 14 | 35 |
| ½ | 1.3 | | 15 | 37.5 |
| ⅝ | 1.6 | | 16 | 40 |
| ¾ | 1.9 | | 17 | 42.5 |
| ⅞ | 2.2 | | 18 | 45 |
| 1 | 2.5 | | 19 | 47.5 |
| 1¼ | 3.1 | | 20 | 50 |
| 1½ | 3.8 | | 21 | 52.5 |
| 1¾ | 4.4 | | 22 | 55 |
| 2 | 5 | | 23 | 57.5 |
| 2½ | 6.25 | | 24 | 60 |
| 3 | 7.5 | | 25 | 62.5 |
| 3½ | 8.8 | | 26 | 65 |
| 4 | 10 | | 27 | 67.5 |
| 4½ | 11.3 | | 28 | 70 |
| 5 | 12.5 | | 29 | 72.5 |
| 5½ | 13.8 | | 30 | 75 |
| 6 | 15 | | 31 | 77.5 |
| 7 | 17.5 | | 32 | 80 |
| 8 | 20 | | 33 | 82.5 |
| 9 | 22.5 | | 34 | 85 |
| 10 | 25 | | 35 | 87.5 |
| 11 | 27.5 | | 36 | 90 |

# metric conversion

# index